Principles
in Practice

The Principles in Practice imprint offers teachers concrete illustrations of effective classroom practices based in NCTE research briefs and policy statements. Each book discusses the research on a specific topic, links the research to an NCTE brief or policy statement, and then demonstrates how those principles come alive in practice: by showcasing actual classroom practices that demonstrate the policies in action; by talking about research in practical, teacher-friendly language; and by offering teachers possibilities for rethinking their own practices in light of the ideas presented in the books. Books within the imprint are grouped in strands, each strand focused on a significant topic of interest.

Adolescent Literacy Strand

Adolescent Literacy at Risk? The Impact of Standards (2009) Rebecca Bowers Sipe

Adolescents and Digital Literacies: Learning Alongside Our Students (2010) Sara Kajder

Adolescent Literacy and the Teaching of Reading: Lessons for Teachers of Literature (2010) Deborah Appleman

Writing in Today's Classrooms Strand

Writing in the Dialogical Classroom: Students and Teachers Responding to the Texts of Their Lives (2011) Bob Fecho

Becoming Writers in the Elementary Classroom: Visions and Decisions (2011) Katie Van Sluys

Writing Instruction in the Culturally Relevant Classroom (2011) Maisha T. Winn and Latrise P. Johnson

Literacy Assessment Strand

Our Better Judgment: Teacher Leadership for Writing Assessment (2012) Chris W. Gallagher and Eric D. Turley

Beyond Standardized Truth: Improving Teaching and Learning through Inquiry-Based Reading Assessment (2012) Scott Filkins

Reading Assessment: Artful Teachers, Successful Students (2013) Diane Stephens, editor

Literacies of the Disciplines Strand

Entering the Conversations: Practicing Literacy in the Disciplines (2014) Patricia Lambert Stock, Trace Schillinger, and Andrew Stock

Real-World Literacies: Disciplinary Teaching in the High School Classroom (2014) Heather Lattimer

Doing and Making Authentic Literacies (2014) Linda Denstaedt, Laura Jane Roop, and Stephen Best

Reading in Today's Classrooms Strand

Connected Reading: Teaching Adolescent Readers in a Digital World (2015) Kristen Hawley Turner and Troy Hicks

Connected Reading

Teaching Adolescent Readers in a Digital World

Kristen Hawley Turner
Fordham University

Troy Hicks
Central Michigan University

National Council of Teachers of English
1111 W. Kenyon Road, Urbana, Illinois 61801-1096

Staff Editor: Bonny Graham
Series Editor: Cathy Fleischer
Interior Design: Victoria Pohlmann
Cover Design: Pat Mayer
Cover Image: Kristen Hawley Turner

NCTE Stock Number: 08376

Library of Congress Cataloging-in-Publication Data

Turner, Kristen Hawley.
   Connected reading : teaching adolescent readers in a digital world / Kristen Hawley Turner, Fordham University, Troy Hicks, Central Michigan University.
        pages cm
   Includes bibliographical references and index.
   ISBN 978-0-8141-0837-6 (pbk.)
  1. Reading (Middle School)—United States. 2. Reading—Computer-assisted instruction. 3. Reading comprehension—United States. 4. Literacy—United States. 5. Computers and literacy—United States. I. Hicks, Troy. II. Title.
   LB1632.T87 2015
   428.4071'2—dc23
                                                                    2014044929

To my mom, Carol Noel Hawley, who taught me how to read—and to write. ~ KmhT

And to my mom, Carol Hicks, who shared her love of books . . . both by reading them to me and inspiring me through her own writing. ~ TH

Contents

Acknowledgments

This book is the result of more than a year of research in middle and high school classrooms, and we are indebted to the teachers who invited us to teach and learn with them. Their enthusiasm to experiment, their honest reflections, and their excellent classroom practice shaped our understanding of Connected Reading. Thank you to Kaitlyn Evans, Heather Hollands, Jeremy Hyler, Aram Kabodian, Lauren King, Amy Laitinen, Rebekah O'Dell, Dawn Reed, Andy Schoenborn, Rebekah Shoaf, Natalie Vazquez, Jenn Wolfe, and Jennifer Zito.

To the students of these teachers we offer our heartfelt thanks—for allowing us to be your teachers, for sharing your reading practices willingly, and for helping us to appreciate your digital lives. Yes, the survey was a bit long . . . but your answers were inspiring.

We also could not have completed such an undertaking without a strong research team, which included Lauren Goldberg and Megan Wallace, students in the Fordham Graduate School of Education, and Pam Zimmerman, transcriptionist extraordinaire.

Kristen's mom, Carol Noel Hawley, read the first full draft of the manuscript and, as always, provided valuable feedback. Michelle Schira Hagerman also commented on early drafts of this work. The feedback from NCTE field reviewers and NCTE staffers Kurt Austin and Bonny Graham guided our final revisions.

Finally, we acknowledge our editor, Cathy Fleischer, who convinced us, with casual conversation over a cup of coffee, that we were the right team to take on this project, and whose unwavering support of and enthusiasm for our research and writing have kept us motivated. Thanks, Cathy. ~Turner and Hooch

Reading Instruction for *All* Students

An NCTE Policy Research Brief

Reading instruction has always been stressed for elementary school students, but today it takes on increased importance for *all* grades. Reports like *Time to Act* and *Reading at Risk* raise concern about a lack of depth in the literacy education of adolescent students and lament a general decline in reading among young adults. The Common Core State Standards (CCSS) for reading state that "all students must be able to comprehend texts of steadily increasing complexity as they progress through school," and studies of literacy point to the rising expectations for reading in both schooling and the workplace.[1] Documents like these indicate that teachers need to help all students become readers, regardless of whether they are in elementary or secondary school, so they can succeed in the information age.

Two terms are circulating in current discussions of reading instruction: textual complexity and close reading. Textual complexity is defined in the CCSS as a three-part entity. It includes *quantitative dimensions* such as word length or frequency, sentence length, and cohesion, all of which can be measured by computer software; *qualitative dimensions* such as levels of meaning, clarity of language, and knowledge demands, all of which require human readers; and *reader-text variables* such as reader motivation, knowledge, and experience, qualities best assessed by teachers who know students and texts.[2] Both the qualitative dimensions and the reader-text variables depend upon the professional judgment of teachers, especially the reader-text variables, because only teachers know students well enough to help them find the best text for the purpose at hand, something "leveling" systems cannot do. Research on student readers and the texts they read confirms the need for teachers to play a key role in matching individual students with specific books at appropriate levels of textual complexity:

What we know about our students as readers:

- Students come to reading tasks with varied prior reading experiences, or prior knowledge, which can support their reading of complex texts.
- Students who are engaged and motivated readers read more often and read more diverse texts than students who are unmotivated by the reading task.
- Students who develop expertise with a particular kind of reading—science fiction or online games, for example—outside of school may not think this kind of reading will be valued by their teachers.[3]

What we know about the texts students read:

- In and out of school, the texts students read vary significantly, from linear text-only books to multimodal textbooks to online hypertexts, each of which places different demands on readers and requires different strategies and approaches to reading.
- Students read texts from a variety of disciplines, so content area literacy is important.

Reading Instruction for *All* Students

- The level of difficulty or complexity in a text is not the only factor students consider in choosing texts; interest and motivation also matter.
- Readability or lexile levels can vary significantly within a single text, so it is important to consider other dimensions of textual complexity.[4]

Close reading has been proposed as the way to help students become effective readers of complex texts, and it can be useful, especially when used alongside other approaches. The difficulty is that close reading can be defined in multiple terms. It can mean searching for hidden meanings, positioning the text as the only reality to be considered, and focusing on formal features. Close reading is also a highly contested term among college English instructors. Critics condemn it for conceptualizing the text as a closed world, for limiting student access, and for emphasizing form over content.[5]

Furthermore, research shows that reading comprehension depends on a more complex approach. Specifically, reading comprehension results from the integration of two models, text-based and situation-based. The text-based model focuses on the way words are organized into sentences, paragraphs, and whole texts. The situation model refers to the meaning that results from integration of the text-based approach with the reader's prior knowledge and goals. Close reading is aligned with the text-based approach, and it encourages students to see meaning as one right answer to be extracted from the text. Close reading is often conflated with providing textual evidence for making a claim about a text, but any approach to reading can insist on warrants for interpretations of texts. By itself, then, close reading cannot ensure that students will develop deep understandings of what they read.[6]

Implications for Instructional Policy

Research-based understandings about students, texts, and reading underlie instructional approaches that support students' learning to read complex texts across grade levels and disciplines. Policymakers need to affirm the value of multiple approaches and support teachers' efforts to adopt instructional practices that call upon a variety of effective strategies, including the following.

- Recognize the role that motivation plays in students' reading by modeling for students how to engage with complex texts that do and do not interest them.
- Engage students in performative reading responses such as gesture, mime, vocal intonation, characterization, and dramatization to enable active construction of meaning and construct a collaborative environment that builds on the strengths of individual students.
- Have students read multiple texts focused on the same topic to improve comprehension through text-to-text connections.
- Foster students' engagement with complex texts by teaching students how different textual purposes, genres, and modes require different strategies for reading.
- Encourage students to choose texts, including non-fiction, for themselves, in addition to assigned ones, to help them see themselves as capable readers who can independently use reading capabilities they learn in class.

Reading Instruction for *All* Students

- Demonstrate, especially at the secondary level, how digital and visual texts including multimodal and multigenre texts require different approaches to reading.
- Connect students' reading of complex texts with their writing about reading and with writing that uses complex texts as models so they will recognize and be able to negotiate many different types of complex texts.
- Develop students' ability to engage in meaningful discussion of the complex texts they read in whole-class, small group, and partner conversations so they can learn to negotiate and comprehend complex texts independently.[7]

When teachers can choose from a range of research-based and theoretically grounded instructional approaches, their students learn how to choose from, apply, and reflect on diverse strategies as they take up the varied purposes, subjects, and genres that present complex challenges for readers. Publishers, as well as policymakers and administrators, play an important role in assuring that teachers have appropriate texts and materials to support effective instruction.

Implications for Policies on Formative Assessment

Research shows that formative assessment enables teachers to draw on their knowledge of the students in their classes in order to adjust instruction over time. Accordingly, educational policy needs to affirm the importance of high-quality formative assessment in reading instruction.[8] Formative assessment of reading can take many forms, as the examples below show:

- Teachers can help students develop awareness of their diverse experiences and knowledge—all of which affect the ways they engage with texts. These include reading experiences in previous grades and in out-of-school spaces. Once students have identified their experiences and knowledge, teachers can help students build on them in approaching complex texts—including when their background experiences and knowledge enhance and/or interfere with their ability to read complex texts.
- Asking students to think aloud as they read complex texts can help teachers identify which instructional supports and interventions will best support readers as they face new reading challenges.
- When teachers have identified students who struggle to remain engaged as they read complex texts, they can assess students' interests in order to provide texts that are more likely to foster student engagement.
- Teachers can assess students' ability to think about their reading and about how different kinds of texts impact their reading. This increased awareness can improve students' ability to read complex texts for various purposes.[9]

Implications for Policies on Professional Learning for Teachers

Reading research shows that educational policy needs to include professional development opportunities that enable teachers to match instructional approaches to diverse

Reading Instruction for *All* Students

student needs. In order to support teachers' ability to draw on a complex set of instructional approaches in service of diverse learner reading outcomes, teachers need frequent and sustained opportunities to learn with one another about the range of instructional supports, interventions, and formative assessments as they emerge from the latest reading research and practice. Opportunities to deepen understanding of topics like those listed below will prepare teachers to help students meet the challenges of textual complexity:

- Broaden the repertoire of approaches to reading instruction, drawing on recent and authenticated research.
- Deepen understanding of which combinations of reading strategies are most effective for achieving a particular instructional goal or addressing the needs of a particular student.
- Learn about how disciplinary distinctions open opportunities and challenges for teaching students to read for varied purposes.
- Develop insight into which reading strategies are effective in all disciplines and which are uniquely suited to specific fields.[10]

Preparing students to read complex texts effectively is one of the most important and most challenging responsibilities of schools. With research-based support from policymakers and administration, teachers can enable students at all grade levels to comprehend, draw evidence from, and compare across a wide variety of complex texts.

Endnotes

1. Carnegie Council on Advancing Adolescent Literacy. (2010). *Time to act: An agenda for advancing adolescent literacy for college and career success.* New York, NY: Carnegie Corporation of New York.

National Endowment for the Arts. (2004). *Reading at risk: A survey of literary reading in America.* Washington, DC: Research Division, National Endowment for the Arts.

Common Core State Standards for English Language Arts & Literacy in History/Social Studies, Science, and Technical Subjects, p. 4. http://www.corestandards.org/assets/CCSSI_ ELA%20Standards.pdf.

2. Common Core State Standards for English Language Arts & Literacy in History/Social Studies, Science, and Technical Subjects. Appendix A: Research supporting key elements of the standards. Glossary of key terms. http://www.corestandards.org/assets/Appendix_A.pdf.

3. McNamara, D. S., Kintsch, E., Songer, N. B., & Kintsch, W. (1996). Are good texts always better? Text coherence, background knowledge, and levels of understanding in learning from text. *Cognition and Instruction, 14*, 1–43.

Venable, G. P. (2003). Confronting complex text: Readability lessons from students with language learning disabilities. *Topics in Language Disorders, 23*(3), 225–240.

Brozo, W. G., Shiel, G., & Topping, K. (2007). Engagement in reading: Lessons learned from three PISA countries. *Journal of Adolescent & Adult Literacy, 51*(4), 304–315.

Kajder, S. (2010). *Adolescents and digital literacies: Learning alongside our students.* Urbana, IL: National Council of Teachers of English.

Reading Instruction for *All* Students

4. Hayles, N. K. (2010). How we read: Close, hyper, machine. *ADE Bulletin*, 22(150), 62–79.

Foorman, B. R., Francis, D. J., Davidson, K. C., Harm, M. W., & Griffin, J. (2009). Variability in text features in six grade 1 basal reading programs. *Scientific Studies of Reading 8* (2), 167–197.

Pitcher, B., & Fang, Z. (2007). Can we trust leveled texts? An examination of their reliability and quality from a linguistic perspective. *Literacy*, 41, 43–51.

5. Student Achievement Partners. Guidelines for developing text-dependent questions for close analytical reading. http:// www.achievethecore.org/steal-these-tools/text-dependent-questions.

Bialostosky, D. (2006). Should college English be close reading? *College English*, 69(2), 111–116.

Murray, H. (1991). Close reading, closed writing. *College English* 53(2), 195–208.

Rabinowitz, P. J. (1992). Against close reading. *Pedagogy Is Politics*. Ed. Maria-Regina Kecht. Chicago: University of Illinois Press.

6. Kintsch, W. (1988). The role of knowledge in discourse comprehension: A construction-integration model. *Psychological Review*, 95, 163–182.

7. Adomat, D. S. (2010). Dramatic interpretations: Performative responses of young children to picture book read-alouds. *Children's Literature in Education*, 41(3), 207–221.

Brozo et al. (2007).

Coiro, J. (2011). Talking about reading as thinking: Modeling the hidden complexities of online reading comprehension. *Theory into Practice* 50(2), 107.

Hayles (2010).

Hiebert, E. H. (2011). The Common Core's staircase of text complexity: Getting the size of the first step right. *Reading Today*, 29(3), 26–27.

Heisey, N., & Kucan, L. (2010). Introducing science concepts to primary students through read-alouds: Interactions and multiple texts make the difference. *The Reading Teacher*, 63(8), 666–676.

Juzwik, M. M., Nystrand, M., Kelly, S., & Sherry, M. B. (2008). Oral narrative genres as dialogic resources for classroom literature study: A contextualized case study of conversational narrative discussion. *American Educational Research Journal*, 45(4), 1111–1154.

Palincsar, A. S., & Schutz, K. M. (2011): Reconnecting strategy instruction with its theoretical roots, *Theory into Practice*, 50(2), 85–92.

Pike, M. M., Barnes, M. A., & Barron, R. W. (2010). The role of illustrations in children's inferential comprehension. *Journal of Experimental Child Psychology*, 105(3).

Quirk, M., Schwanenflugel, P. J., & Webb, M. Y. (2009). A short-term longitudinal study of the relationship between motivation to read and reading fluency skill in second grade. *Journal of Literacy Research*, 41(2).

Tunks, K. W. (2011). Exploring journals as a genre for making reading–writing connections. *Childhood Education*, 87(3), 169.

8. NCTE. (2010). Fostering high-quality formative assessment: A policy brief produced by the National Council of Teachers of English. *The Council Chronicle*, 20(1), 12–15.

Reading Instruction for *All* Students

9. Brown, C. L. (2007). Supporting English language learners in content-reading. *Reading Improvement, 44*(1).

Caldwell, J., & Leslie, L. (2010). Thinking aloud in expository text: Processes and outcomes. *Journal of Literacy Research, 42*(3), 308–340.

Collins, P., Land, R. E., Pearson, M., et al. (2012). Enhancing the interpretive reading and analytical writing of mainstreamed English learners in secondary school: Results from a randomized field trial using a cognitive strategies approach. *American Educational Research Journal, 49*(2), 323–355.

Horning, A. S. (2011). Where to put the manicules: A theory of expert reading. *Across the Disciplines, 8*(2). http://wac.colostate. edu/atd/articles/horning2011/index.cfm.

Little, C. A., & Hines, A. H. (2006). Time to read: Advancing reading achievement after school. *Journal of Advanced Academics, 18*(1), 8–33.

McNamara et al. (1996).

Ramsay, C. M., & Sperling, R. A. (2010). Designating reader perspective to increase comprehension and interest. *Contemporary Educational Psychology, 35*(3), 215–227.

Venable (2003).

10. Herman, J., Hanson, T. L., Boscardin, C. K., et al. (2011). Integrating literacy and science in biology: Teaching and learning impacts of reading apprenticeship professional development. *American Educational Research Journal 48*(3).

Liang, L. A. (2011). Scaffolding middle school students' comprehension and response to short stories. *Research in Middle Level Education Online, 34*(8), 1–16. http://www.nmsa.org/Publications/RMLEOnline/Articles/Vol34No8/tabid/2405/Default. aspx.

This policy brief was produced by NCTE's James R. Squire Office of Policy Research, directed by Anne Ruggles Gere, with assistance from Anne Beatty Martinez, Elizabeth Homan, Danielle Lillge, Justine Neiderhiser, Chris Parsons, Ruth Anna Spooner, Sarah Swofford, and Chinyere Uzogara.

Reimagining Reading Instruction for *All* Students

Chapter One

Who am I as a reader?

As teachers, this is a question we may not ask ourselves very often. When we do, we might immediately think of our favorite kinds of text. Books. Magazines. Blogs. The literary among us might consider a favorite author. Shakespeare. Angelou. Patterson.

Texts and authors have, for good reason, dominated the teaching of English—and our definition of *reading*—for the history of our profession. Because texts came in only a few forms—namely, as printed, bound volumes and periodicals, whether magazines or newspapers—we spent the majority of our time focused on the words themselves. Even though the pages, fonts, colors, and figures used in these publications were all different forms of technology (as stated by Dennis Baron, "Writing itself is always first and foremost a technology, a way of engineering materials in order to accomplish an end" [2001, p. 71]), we very rarely, at least as readers, paused to think about the technology of print.

Then, a little more than a decade after the graphical interface of the World Wide Web rocked our vision of literacy, Amazon's Kindle hit the market in November 2007, and since then our reading lives have never quite been the same. In fact, the 2014 Pew study provides a snapshot of reading in the United States that indicates adults read in a variety of ways (Zickuhr & Rainie, 2014). Though most have not abandoned print reading completely, ownership of handheld devices for reading has grown, with more than 50 percent of adults owning either a tablet or dedicated e-reader.

With this changing landscape, embedded in the question of "who am I as a reader" are the old questions of *who* and *what* we read, as well as new questions of *where* and *how* we read. Turning the pages of a print book, browsing the Internet through mouse clicks, and interacting via fingertips on a tablet's touch screen all represent reading habits in a digital age that are mediated by technology in one form or another. The image in Figure 1.1, captured in the New York City subway by Kristen, shows just one moment in the lives of three readers: one with a magazine, one with a book, and one with a tablet. Similar pictures could be snapped in Troy's home when his children gather to read, one with a downloaded book on an iPad, another with magazines, and yet another with books.

Figure 1.1. Three readers in a New York City subway station.

More than three decades ago, Rosenblatt (1978) encouraged English teachers to think of the process of reading as an interaction between reader, text, and poem. Her transactional theory of reading suggested that we, as readers, had a distinct role in the process of making meaning. While Rosenblatt's approach remains relevant, in addition to the reader, text, and poem, today we must also consider the *device*. What opportunities do smartphones, tablets, e-readers, and computers afford readers? What constraints do they place on readers? How has the introduction of digital texts changed the process of reading?

Specific examples of this change include clicking on a word for its definition, highlighting a favorite passage and posting it to a social network, delving more deeply into a hypertext that demands participation, or downloading an ebook. All of these actions have changed the work we have to do as readers to comprehend texts. You've probably noticed these changes in your own reading, and you also might see how your students interact with digital texts. Although we know that the interaction between a reader and the text has always been a dynamic and contested space (and that texts are not inherently singular nor tied to only one meaning), in this era of digital reading we now must consider a shift to account for the changes in *how* we read. And with these shifts, we also must consider how we teach reading to adolescents.

Of course, paying attention to how teens read is not a new phenomenon. Over the past three decades, teachers and researchers have attended more and more to the specific needs of adolescent readers. From early calls in *A Nation at Risk* (National Commission on Excellence in Education, 1983) to the seminal 1999 position statement from the International Reading Association (revised 2012b), numerous blue-ribbon panels, government reports, manuscripts, books, conferences, and workshops have focused on a variety of techniques to engage, support, and evaluate adolescent readers, including:

- Strategy-based approaches for comprehension (e.g., Beers, 2003; Harvey & Goudvis, 2007; Keene & Zimmermann, 2007; Tovani, 2000, 2004)

- A focus on young adult literature with relatable characters, situations, and themes (e.g., Cart, 2010; Hayn & Kaplan, 2012; Wolf, Coats, Enciso, & Jenkins, 2011)

- Immersive and interactive models of reading instruction such as literature circles and the reading workshop (e.g., Atwell, 2007; Daniels, 2002)

- A renewed attention to content area literacy, which has begun to shift toward disciplinary literacies (e.g., Daniels & Steineke, 2011; Daniels, Zemelman, & Steineke, 2007; Daniels & Zemelman, 2004; Fisher, Brozo, Frey, & Ivey, 2010; Fisher & Frey, 2011; Shanahan & Shanahan, 2008)

Despite these significant efforts, the broad research literature on adolescent literacy has demonstrated a desperate need for English and content area teachers to do even more. Noting the "crisis" type of mentality that permeates the discourse of documents like the Carnegie Council's report on adolescent literacy, "A Time to Act" (Carnegie Corporation of New York's Council on Advancing Adolescent Literacy, 2009), we—Kristen and Troy, as English educators, parents, and the authors of this book—are hesitant to reassert the claim of "crisis." However, we are also hesitant to ignore it.

While many of these lines of literacy research and practice mentioned on page 3 take a sociocultural, constructivist approach—one that honors the lived lives of adolescents, including their skills, interests, and abilities—a considerable gap is emerging in the literature related to digital reading practices. Some researchers, such as Leu, Coiro, and their colleagues, have begun to look at the digital reading practices of adolescents by paying special attention to the types of strategies these students use when searching for and verifying information found on the Internet (Coiro, 2005, 2011; Leu, Kinzer, Coiro, & Cammack, 2004). Others, such as Kajder (2006, 2010) and Kist (2005), have considered broader literacy practices that adolescents employ as active online citizens, reading and writing a variety of texts. Still others have explored the uses of cell phones in school settings (Hyler & Hicks, 2014; Kolb, 2008, 2011; Nielsen & Webb, 2011), the power of blogging and other digital reading and writing tools (Beach, Anson, Breuch, & Swiss, 2008; Hicks, 2009, 2013; Richardson, 2010), and the effects that "digitalk" have had on adolescent literacies (Turner, 2009, 2012, 2014). These lines of thinking are important. However, with the advent of digital reading devices such as smartphones, tablets, and e-readers, even the digital practices documented in the work of these scholars have begun to change in the past few years.

Moreover, the Common Core State Standards (CCSS) demand closer attention to *textual complexity* and *close reading*, two highly contested terms. Reading the CCSS, we see that definitions for these terms include phrases such as "sophistication of what students read and the skill with which they read," "a steadily growing ability to discern more from and make fuller use of text," "critical reading necessary to pick carefully through the staggering amount of information available today in print and digitally," and "wide, deep, and thoughtful engagement with high-quality literary and informational texts that builds knowledge, enlarges experience, and broadens worldviews" (Common Core State Standards Initiative, 2010). Although there has been some confusion about the original intent of these terms, especially *close reading*, Shanahan (2012) notes that

> in the past, the usual practice was to read a text thoroughly a single time in a guided or directed reading lesson. However, the new standards require something different—that students read more challenging texts and engage in "close reading" lessons, in which rereading is a hallmark.

These concerns about close reading and text complexity have become the new currency by which reading programs and instruction are being measured. But this is not happening in an isolated, educational echo chamber.

Nowhere is rereading, attentive reading, or close reading more important than in the various digital contexts in which adolescents read on a daily basis, in part because, many argue, readers do not always read such texts with the same level of attention they pay to print forms. Most famously, Nicholas Carr once asked, "Is Google Making Us Stupid?" (2008). Carr's book *The Shallows: What the Internet Is Doing to Our Brains* (2010) furthered his exploration into that question, and *The Dumbest Generation: How the Digital Age Stupefies Young Americans and Jeopardizes Our Future* (Bauerlein, 2008) answers that question with a resounding "yes." Even noted sociologist Sherry Turkle has critiqued our increasingly networked lives in her latest book, *Alone Together: Why We Expect More from Technology and Less from Each Other* (2011), arguing that the devices we use to mediate our relationships have had an adverse effect on our psyches. These concerns about distractibility, lack of ambition, and a general loss of intellectual engagement with a variety of texts and people can be found in many major media stories across the political spectrum.

We, along with other teachers, researchers, and journalists, are a bit more optimistic about the fate of reading in a digital age. Pushing back against this rhetoric of technological doom, other authors praise Internet technologies for their effect on human connectivity and the resulting collective intelligence. As Clive Thompson argues in his book *Smarter Than You Think* (2013), "Digital tools aren't magical pixie dust that makes you smarter. The opposite is true: they give up the rewards only if you work hard and master them, just like the cognitive tools of previous generations" (p. 73). It is the idea of a *mindful use* of technology that we find most important as adult readers who understand the influence that tools have on us as we make meaning of texts. In fact, as we have gathered data for this book, both on our own reading practices as well as on the reading habits of adolescents, we have redefined for ourselves the idea of "digital" reading. Digital tools, used mindfully, enable connections. Digital reading is connected reading.

We explore this view and specifically the concept of Connected Reading further in Chapter 2, but it is within this broader context that we view reading in a digital age. Simply put, Connected Reading is a model that situates individual readers within a broader reading community and acknowledges a variety of textual forms, both digital and print. These connections have always been present, especially for avid readers who visit libraries, join book clubs, shop at used bookstores, and talk about their latest reads with anyone who will listen. Yet the technology we now have both for reading and for connecting with others shows us, as parents, teacher educators, and researchers, that something is different. In short, we see that readers are *connected* to one another in increasingly useful ways and that they make meaning of what they read in various ways through their connections.

Though we know many readers who still enjoy the feel of a book in their hands, who complain about eyestrain from devices, and who do not like to read on-screen, we recognize that this is a key part of our reading futures. Or, as the National Writing Project argues, "Quite simply, *digital* is" (2010, p. ix). Because *digital* now defines spaces in which adolescent readers work on a daily basis, we wondered about *what*, *why*, and *how* teens read in their digital lives outside of school.

The Importance of "Digital"

Before we underscore the importance of digital forms of text, we view reading in the twenty-first century not as an either/or, but instead a both/and; we need and want students to read traditional print texts as well as digital texts. We are concerned, however, that the *digital* gets lost in discussions of reform, policy, and implementation. And, if we are being totally honest about it, we wonder if teaching students to read digital texts, specifically, has been marginalized in classroom instruction, too. Even our colleagues who use technology regularly and for purposeful learning in their classrooms have told us that, sadly, they don't spend much time teaching the skills needed for students to comprehend digital texts. For these reasons, we focus our examination of the NCTE policy research brief *Reading Instruction for* All *Students* on reading *digitally* and consider what the brief means for instruction when read from that lens.

A quick note before we dig into the policy statement itself. As collaborators who live in different parts of the country, we rely on digital tools to allow us to read, think, and write together. Our own literacy practices help us to understand the power of digital tools for connecting individuals, and throughout this book we share examples of our practices. Figure 1.2 is a screenshot of our annotation of the NCTE policy statement. It is interesting to note how this particular text came to us and—as one example of how we employ principles of Connected Reading—how we came to make meaning from it.

Like many of you reading this book, we are members of the National Council of Teachers of English (NCTE), and we first encountered this policy statement in print in the organization's September 2012 *Council Chronicle* magazine. At about the same time, we received NCTE's INBOX email newsletter with a link to the PDF. Thus, we had an initial encounter with the text, both in print and on screen. Then our relationship with the document changed. In November 2012, Cathy Fleischer, our editor, handed each of us a printed copy of the statement at our initial, exploratory meeting for this book. Having that photocopy in front of us

Figure 1.2. Our annotations of the NCTE policy research brief via Crocodoc.

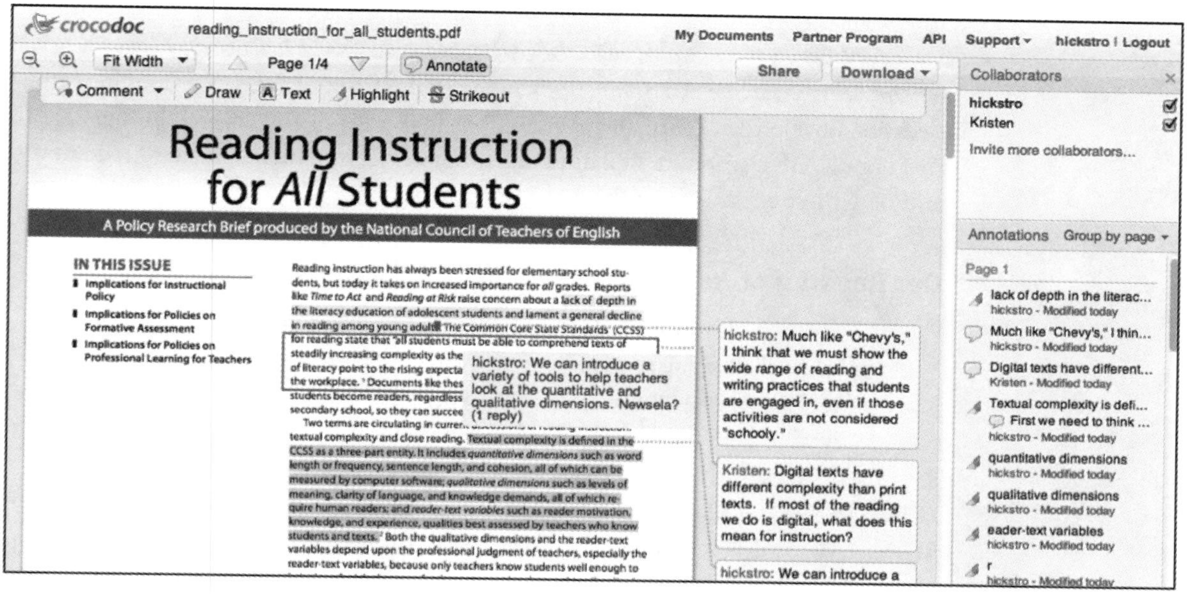

was helpful for the moment, and we each made some notes on our copies, yet we quickly turned our reading digital.

Again, because we are distant collaborators (though we admit that, even if we were in closer geographic proximity, we would choose to use this tool for a variety of reasons), we moved a version of the policy statement onto Crocodoc (http://personal.crocodoc.com). We share Figure 1.2 to demonstrate this one tool used for our shared reading to make a more powerful point: reading need not be isolating. We used Crocodoc both to add personal annotations as well as to engage in dialogue around the policy statement. Crocodoc was not the only tool we could have chosen, of course, but for this particular task, at that particular moment, it allowed us to be connected readers in many useful ways.

The National Writing Project (2010) made this point in relation to digital writing, an act of production that refers to *"compositions created with, and often times for reading or viewing on, a computer or other device that is connected to the Internet"* (p. 7, emphasis in original). Likewise, reading can be an act of collaboration. Readers frequently discuss reading when in face-to-face conversation with one another, often as a pre-, during-, or postreading act. Why not work online throughout the process? Collaboration can happen across distance and time in a way that was not possible before the introduction of digital tools, highlighting the social, connected aspects of reading. This is what Figure 1.2 represents: a shared, collaborative reading experience that could not have happened without digital tools. This is the heart of Connected Reading and what we hope you will carry with you from this book into your classroom.

We now invite you to read, or perhaps reread, NCTE's policy research brief *Reading Instruction for All Students*, included at the front of this book (and hereafter occasionally cited as *RIAS*; all page citations map to the brief's page numbers in this book). Then we share our thinking about key components of the statement and how these ideas inform the rest of the book.

Our Reading of *Reading Instruction for All Students*

> Preparing students to read complex texts effectively is one of the most important and most challenging responsibilities of schools. With research-based support from policymakers and administration, teachers can enable students at all grade levels to comprehend, draw evidence from, and compare across a wide variety of complex texts. (*RIAS*, p. xiv)

The final words of the policy statement articulate what Kristen's mentor, Michael W. Smith, would call "the heart of the matter." As one of the foundational pillars of literacy, reading instruction must focus on multiple goals: developing comprehension, analysis, and comparative skills. The introduction to the document suggests that building these skills is more important than ever before in order for students to "succeed in the information age" (p. xi). We agree, and we offer here our interpretation of the brief through the exploration of six key ideas: (1) text complexity, (2) student readers, (3) close reading, (4) implications for instructional policies, (5) implications for policies on formative assessment, and (6) implications for professional learning for teachers. Though we acknowledge that multiple conversations may evolve from readings of this brief, we narrow our analysis to what the statement means when we think about *digital* reading, or reading text on a screen.

Component 1: Text Complexity

"Text complexity" is a popular phrase that may be echoed in staff development sessions and conversations about policy without much consideration for what the term actually means. The CCSS define *text complexity* in three parts: (1) qualitative dimensions, (2) quantitative dimensions, and (3) reader and task considerations (CCSS Initiative, 2010, Appendix A, p. 4). As we consider text complexity, we focus on the first two of these components in order to make clear the distinction between digital and print versions of texts and to explicitly counter recent interpretations of textual complexity under the CCSS that have omitted differences among students and the various contexts of readers. We discuss students as readers as a separate component of the policy brief.

As teachers of English who believe that reading is an active process by which individual readers make meaning through their interactions with a text and other readers, we have been somewhat baffled by suggestions that students read in terms of "Lexile levels" and that Lexile levels are a fail-safe indication of text complexity. The idea that *Diary of a Wimpy Kid*, as great a book as it is, has more text complexity than a book by Ray Bradbury is, well, ridiculous (Miller, 2012). This argument about Lexile levels is not new (see, for example, Krashen, 2002), yet the overwhelming perception of text complexity as described by advocates for the CCSS is based in quantitative measures of a text. The policy brief helps us to understand why there has been this shift in view away from decades of research that supports other forms of reading assessment beyond Lexile levels.

As we read the policy statement and delineate between *quantitative* and *qualitative* dimensions of the text, we wonder how the authors of the CCSS considered (or, more likely, failed to consider) digital texts when defining *text complexity*, and we fear that interpretations of the standards have negated screen-based texts that provide possibilities for interaction that lead to multiple paths for a reader. How are embedded videos measured in terms of Lexile levels? When a student moves from one webpage to another via a hyperlink, what quantitative dimensions should be measured? Can we measure multimodal texts in the same ways we measure print-based texts? Probably not, because only the reader knows the path that he or she will take, and that is a path constructed during the reading process. We cannot prepare multiple-choice tests for authentic digital reading.

RIAS reminds us that both qualitative and quantitative dimensions of a text are important. We believe that quantitative dimensions of textual complexity, as measured by Lexiles (flawed as they are), speak more to individual texts that are read in a linear fashion. Because of the networked links embedded in many digital texts, digital reading is rarely linear reading, and the choices a reader makes may require knowledge demands beyond those needed to comprehend print texts. For digital texts, qualitative dimensions—including links to additional content and multimedia embedded in the original text—are even more important to comprehension, and thus we need to complicate what is meant by the words *text complexity*, particularly those commonly used quantitative measures.

Component 2: Student Readers

The policy statement makes it clear that student readers vary in their experiences, knowledge, motivation, and text expertise. These youth read a variety of texts—from linear, print books to multimodal and hypertexts—that span disciplines and engage their interests. In many ways, the policy statement stands in stark contrast to the CCSS in which teen readers, in particular, are pigeon-holed. Even though the CCSS focus on reading a variety of texts across disciplines, the list of canonical texts in the CCSS appendix limits the types of literature that might be read. By neglecting interest-driven reading, a powerful motivator for adolescents, and especially by forgoing significant conversation about reading done in digital spaces, the writers of the CCSS have made some assumptions about adolescents in a digital age, and we believe *what* and *how* teens read in digital venues is an area of research that has been neglected.

Component 3: Close Reading

Again, definitions of *close reading* vary. Lehman and Roberts (2014), for instance, describe close reading as "careful meditation on texts" (p. 3) and remind us of the roots of close reading. They argue that "reading closely, then, was the process of trying to tune out everything else while looking at the style, words, meter, structure, and so on, of a piece of writing—letting the text itself shine through" (p. 2). While paying particular attention to the text, and highlighting this one aspect of New Criticism as a literary theory, close reading in this sense suggests that we can draw meaning from the words on the page without making connections to other texts or our own prior knowledge.

Timothy Shanahan describes it this way:

> Close reading requires a substantial emphasis on readers figuring out a high quality text. This "figuring out" is accomplished primarily by reading and discussing the text (as opposed to being told about the text by a teacher or being informed about it through some textbook commentary). Because challenging texts do not give up their meanings easily, it is essential that readers re-read such texts (not all texts are worth close reading). (Shanahan, 2012)

Additional definitions of *close reading* include "disciplined reading . . . with a view to deeper understanding" (Brummett, 2009, p. 9) and attending closely to the interactions among personal thoughts, the responses of other readers, and "close attention to the text" (Beers & Probst, 2012, p. 37). The policy brief explains that the term itself is "highly contested" (*RIAS*, p. xii), yet we recognize that *close reading* has entered our instructional lexicon, and we must address it in productive and responsible ways.

The policy statement offers this advice: "Close reading has been proposed as *the* way to help students become effective readers of complex texts, and it can be useful, especially *when used alongside other approaches*" (*RIAS*, p. xii, emphasis added). We have highlighted words in this excerpt from the policy statement that capture both the essence of the problem of close reading in conversations about reading instruction, as well as the solution to this problem that is presented by the brief. Educational debates often present themselves as either/or dichotomies: whole language vs. phonics; fiction vs. nonfiction; writing across the curriculum vs. writing in disciplines. As we have learned time and again, these debates are rarely either/or, and answers are most often contextualized, lying somewhere on a continuum.

The research brief points out that close reading has—at least in popular discourse—become *the* answer to questions about how to teach students to read complex texts. But as with all instruction, there is not one correct answer. Rather, the policy statement reminds us that close reading is one of many tools teachers can use to help students improve their comprehension, analysis, and comparative skills.

We find this reminder particularly important when considering digital texts. If, as the brief states, "close reading is aligned with the text-based approach" to reading and "it encourages students to see meaning as one right answer to be extracted from the text" (*RIAS*, p. xii), we wonder how we *could* do a close read on a digital, hyperlinked text. In some ways, many digital texts continue infinitely, each one connected to another through a vast network of links. These kinds of texts invite individual exploration. Readers follow their own paths. Furthermore, the vast amount of linked text requires skills of sifting and sorting of information simply to decide where and when a close reading is required. Are these skills part of a close reading process? Is participation—including reading, sharing, and connecting—required in order to closely read digital texts?

Conversations about close reading make us uncomfortable because they often focus solely on print-based, linear texts. As the authors of the brief suggest, "By itself, then, close reading cannot ensure that students will develop deep understandings of what they read" (*RIAS*, p. xii), particularly, we would suggest, when they read digital texts.

Component 4: Implications for Instructional Policies

In our conversations with fellow teachers, we often see a divide between print and digital literacy, and we personally believe the CCSS do not go far enough to transform understandings of literacy to align with the real demands of college and the workplace today. However, as we consider the list of instructional strategies in the policy statement, we are encouraged. NCTE, as it always has, continues to push toward more engaging, inclusive, and interpretive methods of teaching. We summarize their suggested strategies here:

- Recognize the role of motivation
- Engage in performative response
- Read multiple texts
- Foster engagement
- Encourage choice
- Demonstrate differences in digital and visual texts
- Connect reading and writing
- Develop meaningful discussion

Rather than simply imparting the meaning of a text on students, the strategies here confirm what decades of research have shown about the moves that effective teachers of reading make for and with their students. As the word cloud in Figure 1.3 shows, all the language from the policy statement's bullet points that focus on instructional strategies add up to indicate that students are at the center of instruction.

We also see embedded in these points a number of references to Connected Reading of digital texts that acknowledge the shift society has made. And when shown in such a stark manner, we see great potential for teaching Connected Reading practices and for engaging all readers using digital tools.

Figure 1.3. Word cloud of implications for instructional practice from NCTE's policy research brief *Reading Instruction for All Students* (created with Wordle.net).

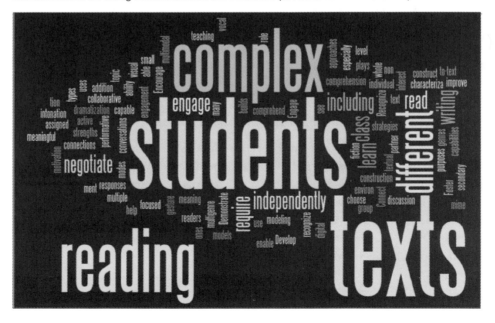

Component 5: Implications for Policies on Formative Assessment

By the time this book is published, it is most likely that the PARCC and SBAC assessments will have become the default standardized tests in your state; even if your state is not participating in the CCSS adoption, your students will still likely be taking their reading tests on a computer.

We want to be clear here. From what we have seen of the Partnership for Assessment of Readiness for College and Careers (PARCC) and Smarter Balanced Assessment Consortium (SBAC) model assessments, these are not tests of digital reading, at least not as we define digital, Connected Reading in this book. Nor are these tests representative of formative assessment of reading as it is defined in the NCTE policy research brief. The brief makes clear that formative assessment focuses on process and on identifying strengths and areas for improvement of individual novice readers. Tracking Lexile levels and comparing reading scores to an arbitrary line of proficiency do little to connect assessment and instruction, a link important for both formative assessment and the development of readers. Still, we believe that digital tools have potential to make formative assessments possible by providing immediate feedback to readers and teachers. We discuss many of these tools in this book and demonstrate how to use these tools in ways to support Connected Reading, not just proficiency testing.

Component 6: Implications for Professional Learning for Teachers

The policy brief closes with implications for professional learning that highlight the need to focus on research-based practices, as compared to policy-driven reactions. The suggestions underscore the importance of context in reading. We agree that context is always important; we argue that digital contexts must be included in these conversations. This book is our attempt to expand the professional conversation about reading instruction to include the reading of digital texts. To meet students where they are and to help them become critical readers of various kinds of texts, both print and digital, teachers must understand the out-of-school reading practices in which their students engage. We cannot assume that adolescents today are "digital natives" (Prensky, 2001) who naturally gain close reading skills on a screen. Most of the teachers with whom we have worked would agree: a smartphone does not a smart reader make. We need to understand *what* it means to read digitally, *how* students read, and *why* they choose the digital texts they do in order to help them develop their comprehension, analytic, and comparative skills.

Our Approach in This Book

As you can see, our reading of the policy brief raises questions for us, and we come to this task with a broad interest in teaching reading. We are, after all, teachers of

English, lovers of fiction and nonfiction, poetry and prose. Both of us find pleasure in reading to our own children and in teaching teachers how to better teach literacy practices to their students. We are also writers who care deeply about the connections between reading and writing, particularly in a digital age.

Additionally, we approach our questions as qualitative researchers, and over the past year we have drawn on appropriate methodological tools and dispositions to explore the digital reading practices of adolescents. We have worked closely with teachers whose classrooms (grades 7–12) are highlighted throughout this book. We have each taught lessons on digital reading, described in Chapters 5 and 6, in these classrooms. We have collected more than 800 responses to a survey that we created on digital reading habits, and we have interviewed twenty-three adolescents about their reading practices.

Our field research has generated lots of data, and the stories you will read in this book are our best attempt to paint an accurate picture of what is really happening with teachers and students in a variety of contexts. We provide a more detailed description of our research method in Appendix A. But it is important to articulate our stance related to technology—and specifically teens' access to digital devices and the Internet—before we dive into the chapters. We modeled our Digital Reading Survey (see Appendix B) on the "Teen Parent Survey on Writing" used by the Pew Internet & American Life Project for their work related to *Writing, Technology and Teens* (Lenhart, Arafeh, Smith, & Macgill, 2008). The Pew survey asked questions about the kinds of devices that teens possessed five years ago, including dial-up modems. Pew, of course, has updated its surveys and results since then, and we report their updated data, as well as our own, in Table 1.1 in the following section.

Do My Students Have Access to the Internet and Devices?

We have both worked with teachers in a variety of contexts, especially in conferences and workshops, and we are often reminded of their concerns about students' access to technology, both inside and outside of school. In fact, access to technology is one of the biggest "yeah, but . . ." reasons we hear for teachers being unable to implement digital literacies into their classrooms. We have argued recently that, as a profession, we need to move beyond these hesitancies to consider the implications (and consequences) of *not* teaching specific skills of digital writing and digital reading (Hicks & Turner, 2013). We recognize that, for some students, the digital divide is still very real. Yet, as Pew Internet data have demonstrated and our research confirms, a vast majority of students do indeed have access in some way. Throughout this book, we highlight the voices of individuals, as well as shared statistics of the larger group that we surveyed.

We distributed an electronic survey to middle and high school students in the states of California, Michigan, New Jersey, and New York. We admit we did not collect a randomized, representative sample in the statistical sense since we were working with students in the classrooms of teachers we knew. In this sense, we see the limitation of our study. Still, we want to make clear that these students come from a variety of schools and a variety of backgrounds: rural, suburban, urban; lower-, middle-, and upper-class incomes.

Of the 804 respondents to our survey, 76 percent say they use the Internet several times a day, and another 11 percent report using it about once a day. In total, 87 percent of the students use the Internet *every day*. The remaining 13 percent use it from one to five times a week. This Internet use is not surprising in light of the fact that 94 percent of students access it from a wireless or mobile device, which they, presumably, carry with them much of the time. In fact, these teenagers have many devices, as shown in Table 1.1.

Given the large number of students who report that they own wireless handheld devices, we were interested in the breakdown of these data, particularly for those students who do not access the Internet daily. Of the 13 percent who said they do not access the Internet daily, 69 percent said they access it the *most* at home, indicating that their homes do have either wireless or hardwire connections even if they are not using them daily. Also of that same 13 percent, 55 percent reported owning a smartphone. Of those who do not own a smartphone, 65 percent own a wireless handheld device.

Table 1.1. Device Ownership of Teenagers for Connected Reading Sample Compared to Previous Research from Pew Internet & American Life Project

	Connected Reading (data we collected from 2013: 804 teens)	**Pew Study** (data from 2012: 802 parents and 802 teens
Daily Internet Use	87%	95%
Mobile Phone	84%	78%
Smartphone	71%	37%
Internet-Enabled Handheld Device (e.g., iPod Touch)	71%	N/A
Laptop or Desktop at Home	77%	93%
e-Reader	21% dedicated e-reader 45% Internet enabled	N/A

To take a different look at these statistics, imagine that you have 100 students on your roster throughout the day. To begin, 87 of them can and do access the Internet daily on a variety of devices. Another 7, though they do not go online daily, own a smartphone and, while it isn't quite the same as having a laptop or tablet that allows them to see a larger screen, they do have access either through their cell provider or open wireless networks. (At this point, 94 total students have access.) Four more have a wireless-enabled device that can also be used on open wireless networks such those as at malls, restaurants, and libraries. Now we are at 98 total. The remaining 2 students, according to our data, access the Internet at someone else's home or from a public library. From our survey results, it appears as though all 100 of your students would have some kind of regular access to the Internet, even if it is not on a daily basis at home.

We know there are outliers to these data and that for some students access is an issue. But now that we can report with our own data that the Pew numbers cited in Table 1.1 are accurate, we feel that teachers' concerns that they "can't expect students to do work online" can be lessened, if not completely abated. Therefore, it bears repeating: more than two-thirds of our students have access to the Internet via mobile phone. Nearly nine out of ten report using the Internet at least once every day. We can and should expect students to use the Internet by teaching them the digital literacy skills necessary to use that access in smart, academically appropriate ways. So we approach this book with the belief that issues of access can—and must—be overcome. The data bear it out: students have access to the Internet. But does our mindset about teaching with the Internet align with the data? Teaching your students to be Connected Readers will help them make the case for why they should spend their time online engaging in texts and sharing their ideas with others.

Overview of the Book

Like all the books in the Principles in Practice imprint, the chapters here delve deeper into an NCTE policy statement. In particular, we aim to accomplish at least three goals as we examine *Reading Instruction for* All *Students*.

1. To further unpack the policy statement by providing real examples of what teachers are teaching and students are doing as readers

2. To explore the idea of digital reading and to offer a model of Connected Reading that has developed from our analysis of what readers in digital contexts do

3. To provide, as accurately as possible, a series of snapshots of who adolescent readers are and how they select and respond to texts, both in school and out, as reading practices shift to more and more digital devices

We begin in Chapter 2 by rethinking reading in a digital age. We share our model of Connected Reading and outline how other theory and research contribute to our thinking.

In Chapter 3, we offer reflections on our own reading practices, coupled with profiles of a few of the students we interviewed. Through these glimpses into readers' worlds, we articulate (1) the kinds of digital texts that readers encounter and (2) the practices that readers of digital texts engage with.

Chapter 4 further explores the model of Connected Reading through the readers in our study. Reporting data from both the interviews and the survey, we paint a portrait of adolescent readers' complex reading practices as influenced by digital devices, as well as their relationship with print media.

As our research uncovered unequivocally, print texts still exist and still have value in our students' reading lives. In Chapter 5, however, we offer ideas for teachers to augment instruction of print texts using digital tools to develop Connected Readers. We highlight the work we did with teachers and their students over the last year, focusing specifically on using Connected Reading principles to support classroom instruction with print-based texts.

Chapter 6 looks closely at developing Connected Reading practices with digital texts, and again, we share lessons that we developed with teachers and taught to their students.

Chapter 7 reflects once again on the policy statement, considering implications for Connected Reading instruction and assessment.

Finally, in Chapter 8 we suggest that an inquiry stance is needed to fully realize and implement Connected Reading instruction.

Also, as we mention later in the book, you can find our companion wiki site containing additional resources and discussions available at http://connectedreading.wiki spaces.com (see Figure 1.4). If you are using a mobile device, you can scan this QR code and go directly to the wiki. In the writing of this book—even during final copy-editing—we learned of new tools that would be useful for both readers and teachers alike. Our wiki showcases  resources that become available even after the book has been printed.

We also want to make it clear that this book aims to offer a critical, careful look at the benefits and drawbacks of digital reading. We hear terms such as *digital natives, millennials,* and *screenagers,* and we wince just a little bit. These terms, as all stereotypes do, very much oversimplify an entire generation of students. Yes, as many surveys, including our own, demonstrate, the vast majority of these students have smartphones, tablets, and varying yet usually adequate Internet access. These readers are diverse, however, and they range in their engagement, their connectedness, and their digital reading practices. You, as their English teacher, are a key link to helping them comprehend, respond to, and critique digital texts, just as you have always been for print texts.

We do not buy into the dominant narratives circulated in the media about a literacy crisis, yet we do acknowledge that we have many kinds of readers in our classrooms, all of whom are wonderfully complicated adolescents, each with his or her own interests, needs, and, preferences for when, where, what, why, and how to read. You know these students too, and you understand that we must teach them how to read, not simply expect that they can read. While some excel, many do not, and our work is helping them become better readers. Similarly, some of our students are Connected Readers, and we appreciate what they have shared with us in this study. However, many are not, and we hope that this book offers you guidance as you begin teaching Connected Reading in your own classroom.

Figure 1.4. Homepage of the Connected Reading wiki.

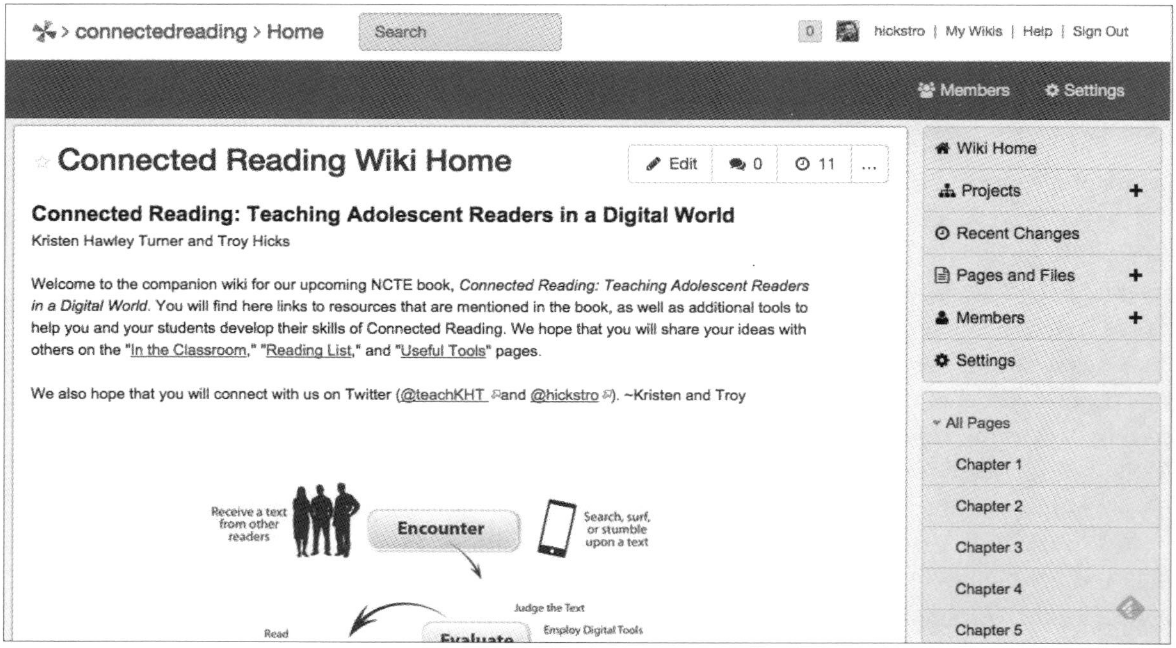

Rethinking Comprehension in a Digital Age: Connected Reading

We began writing this book with questions about teenagers and their digital reading practices:

- What do they read?
- How do they use devices?
- Why do they choose the digital texts they do?
- What types of strategies do they use to engage with texts?

To explore these questions, we worked with twelve middle and high school teachers during the spring of the 2012–13 school year and the fall of the 2013–14 school year. We make specific reference to the year because we acknowledge that in the changing landscape of digital literacies, data such as the kind we report here are never fixed. Still, the data related to technology use and access that we share in Chapter 1 continue a trend in research that suggests that device ownership and access to the Internet continue to rise each year.

Remember that all links and handouts are located on the companion wiki. Scan this QR code or go to http://connectedreading.wikispaces.com to access Chapter 2 materials.

We collected these data in a variety of grades 7–12 classrooms in California, Michigan, New Jersey, and New York as we asked adolescents to reflect on their reading practices and taught lessons related to digital reading. Though we approached aspects of data collection and analysis as qualitative researchers, we also acted as participants in the classrooms, each of us teaching one or more lessons related to digital literacy, often for two or three consecutive days or across an entire unit of study (see Appendix A for a description of our research methodology). Thus, while neither of us teaches in a 7–12 classroom on a daily basis, we attempted in our research and the writing of the book to accurately reflect what it means for *you* to teach reading in a digital age. It is difficult work, no doubt, yet we are excited about what the future of reading holds for all of us, especially your students.

Our work over the course of ten months of data collection and analysis led us to our model of Connected Reading, and this chapter explains this model, its features, and its relationship to a rich tradition of research and theory in the field of literacy instruction.

Connected Reading: An Emerging Model of Reading Comprehension in a Digital World

Our research began with a focus on *what*, *how*, and *why* teens read digitally, yet the study was embedded in a rich tradition of research on reading instruction specifically and literacy practices broadly. Given the history of the field, we understand the process of "reading" to be one that is complicated by many factors. We know that readers bring to texts both experiences and skills that will shape their interpretations. We know that motivation and interest matter. And we know that the difficulty of a text, or the specific textual features present, will affect the process of comprehension.

However, we also know that the number of choices that readers in a digital world must make with any particular text is growing exponentially. Texts come in many forms, and contexts for reading are shaped by a network of other readers. To account for the growing number of texts available to readers (in both quantity and types) and the complicated decisions associated with reading them, we present in Figure 2.1 a model of Connected Reading in a Digital Age.

We hope you notice two key features of the model. First, it is not linear, and second, multiple readers are represented. These features get at the heart of what readers do in a digital world. They are connected to one another through a network, receiving and sharing texts according to purpose and context, and their processes are recursive.

Figure 2.1. Connected Reading model.

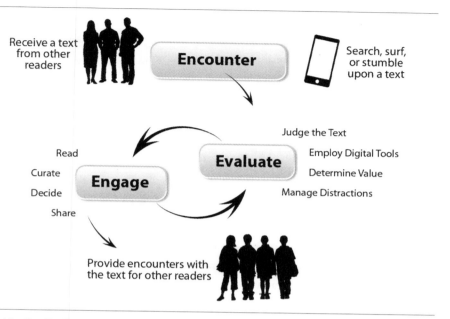

We identify three primary practices of Connected Readers, each of which can be broken down into subpractices that we discuss in detail in the next two chapters:

- Encountering—the manner in which a reader will first make contact with a text. Teens in our research described at least four practices for initially encountering a text, including receiving, searching, surfing, and stumbling.

- Engaging—the activities that happen before, during, and after a reader reads a text. Again, teens shared a variety of actions that we have condensed into acts of deciding, curating, reading, and sharing.

- Evaluating—the act of finding value in a text. In this sense, we refer to evaluation not in the typical sense that it is used in school (to place judgment upon, as a grade) but in the sense that a reader can find various types of value in a text. In other words, how important is this text to this reader? In the process of evaluation, teens would consider their overall interest, critique the text itself, employ digital tools to engage with the text, and choose to manage distraction (or not) based on how much they valued the text.

Evaluating and engaging, in particular, do not happen in isolated stages; rather, readers constantly evaluate as they decide, curate, read, and share.

Theoretical Influences of Connected Reading

Although our analysis of the data led to this model of Connected Reading, we acknowledge here several lines of research that frame our study and help us to understand "what readers do" in a digital age. Given that this text, like others in the PIP imprint, is devoted to thinking about classroom practice, we don't delve too deeply into theory here. However, we know that effective practice is informed by theory and research. Therefore, we want to alert you that the next sections move into some theoretical influences that have guided our thinking in this research project and while writing the book.

Reading as Socially (and Digitally) Situated

Readers draw on strategies for comprehension that have been documented by a rich tradition of research into reading with print texts. Beginning with the work of P. David Pearson in the late 1970s (Pearson & Johnson, 1978) and stretching right up to the present day, literacy researchers and teachers have continued to refine a list of strategies through which good readers engage before, during, and after the act of reading. Most notably, researchers and teachers who support a view of strategy-based approaches for comprehension describe activities for monitoring comprehension, activating prior knowledge, asking questions, inferring, visualizing, determining importance, summarizing, and synthesizing (Beers, 2003; Harvey & Goudvis, 2007; Keene & Zimmermann, 2007; Tovani, 2000, 2004). These activities feed into broader models of reading instruction, such as literature circles and the reading workshop (Atwell, 2007; Daniels, 2002) and increased attention to content area and disciplinary literacy (Daniels & Steineke, 2011; Daniels et al., 2007; Daniels & Zemelman, 2004; Fisher et al., 2010; Fisher & Frey, 2011;

Theoretical Influence: Reading Strategies

Before Reading	During Reading	After Reading
Activate prior knowledge	Infer meaning	Summarize
Preview the text	Visualize	Synthesize
Examine text features	Determine importance	Create citations
Ask questions	Make connections	Choose new texts
	Ask questions	

Jetton & Shanahan, 2012). Comprehension strategy instruction helps make reading practices visible, and much of the work in this area is based on what we know about what expert readers do. We have come to understand that although research into New Literacies suggests that some of these traditional strategies may be transferable to digital texts, reading online, particularly with hyperlinked texts, requires additional strategies.

Theoretical Models and Processes of Reading, now in its sixth edition, has been the International Reading Association's flagship publication for decades, documenting the latest scholarship in the field and outlining various approaches for conceptualizing the reading process. In the fifth edition, Leu et al. (2004) write about the changing nature of literacy and outline what it means to move between broad ideas of reading in a world dominated by Internet communication (what they identify throughout the chapter as a "New Literacies Perspective") and specific literacy practices such as texting, collaborating on a document, or building a website (again, identified throughout the chapter with a lowercase "new literacies"). In short, they talk about the effects of Internet-based reading in terms of theoretical shifts in reading practice (New Literacies) and the actual skills a person uses (new literacies). In particular, they outline eight central principles to a New Literacies Perspective:

1. The Internet is this generation's defining technology for literacy and learning within our global community.

2. The Internet and related technologies require additional new literacies to fully access their potential.

3. New literacies are deictic [contextual].

Theoretical Influence: New Literacies

Key Considerations Related to the Reader	Key Considerations Related to the Text
• Existing skills and dispositions toward reading ebooks and online	• Format of the text (webpage, app-based, PDF, ebook)
• Exposure to explicit instruction for digital reading	• Access to the text (free on the Web, available on the "deep Web"/databases, paid ebook or website subscription
• Attention span, ability to avoid distraction, and "mindfulness"	• Can be text only, text with links, multimodal, or fully interactive
• Willingness to participate in social practices related to digital reading	

4. New literacies are multiple, multimodal, and multifaceted.

5. Critical literacies are central to new literacies.

6. New forms of strategic knowledge are required with new literacies.

7. New social practices are a central element of New Literacies.

8. Teachers become more important, though their role changes, within new literacy classrooms. (p. 1589)

In reviewing this list of principles, we offer a brief elaboration on number three: "New literacies are deictic." Leu and colleagues describe how linguists use this Greek word to "define words whose meanings change rapidly as their context changes" (2004, p. 1591). New Literacies, they contend, change every day as newer technologies and social practices enabled by those technologies emerge.

Technologies sometimes change the features of the texts themselves. As a part of comprehension strategy instruction, there are various textual features—table of contents, headings, figures, captions, glossaries, indexes, keywords, and call-out boxes—of which our students need to be made aware. That is, we need to explicitly teach textual features as a way to enhance meaning making. These text features are fairly obvious in print texts; reading on a screen, especially a text that is connected to the Internet, complicates the issue.

Specifically, and to paraphrase one of our student interviewees, digital reading is defined by all those darn links. *Hypertext*, as defined by Wikipedia, is "text displayed on a computer display or other electronic device with references (hyperlinks) to other text which the reader can immediately access, or where text can be revealed progressively at multiple levels of detail" ("Hypertext," 2013). Since the 1970s, a variety of hypertext forms have been introduced, though educators are probably most familiar with the World Wide Web. While print text invites a reader to engage with it, hypertext, by its very nature, demands participation.

Theoretical Influence: Text and Hypertext Features

Print-Based Text Features	Hypertextual Features
• Headings and subheadings	• Links (internal and external)
• Figures, charts, or other visuals	• Site map and organization
• Font styles, including boldface	• Interactive graphics
• Table of contents and indexes	• Audio and video components

A growing body of hypertext literary theory has emerged over the past three decades. Much like the rich tradition of literary theory related to print texts (see, for example, Eagleton, 2008), there are scholars who have continued to push the field in thinking about how hypertext works, as well as what it means. Though beyond the scope of this book to explore fully, a major thinker such as Bolter (2001) can help us see hypertext both as a familiar form (letters, words, sentences, and paragraphs) and in an entirely new way as we make choices as writers about which words to create as hyperlinks—and as readers, which links to follow. These are choices our students are faced with constantly in their own digital reading practices, so becoming conscious of these choices is imperative.

Thus, Connected Reading takes into account the changing nature of texts and the literacies needed to comprehend them. Though reading was never simply *just* about picking up a particular book, New Literacies suggests that the ways that we find, access, interact with, and socialize with text require additional "forms of strategic knowledge" (Leu et al., 2004, p. 1589).

While readers employ various strategies to make meaning, we also know that readers are influenced by other attributes, contexts, and text features. Though choices in where and when to read, previous experiences and skills, and specific textual features influence readers on an individual basis, reading is, in our view, social. Individual readers are connected to other readers before, during, after, and in-between reading events.

The social aspect of reading, while not entirely new, is at least decidedly *different* in an era when opportunities to share and discuss reading become more widely available with mobile technologies. The Connected Learning principles (Figure 2.2) proposed by Ito et al. (2013) help us to think about the production and distribution of knowledge and ideas, especially those related to what we (and our students) read.

As we consider reading instruction for all students, we want to broaden the scope of our thinking about what and why students read, as well as when, where, and how they read. We understand that "students [will] learn how to choose from, apply, and reflect on diverse strategies as they take up the varied purposes, subjects, and genres that present complex challenges" (*RIAS*, p. xiii). We also understand that it would be naive to think that the only kinds of texts they might take up for consideration would be ones we present them with in school, or those they can find only in print. In other words, as students become more proficient and engaged readers, we expect that they will read more texts. Increasingly, their ability to find and engage in these texts has moved online.

Figure 2.2. Connected learning principles infographic (used with permission by Attribution Creative Commons License).

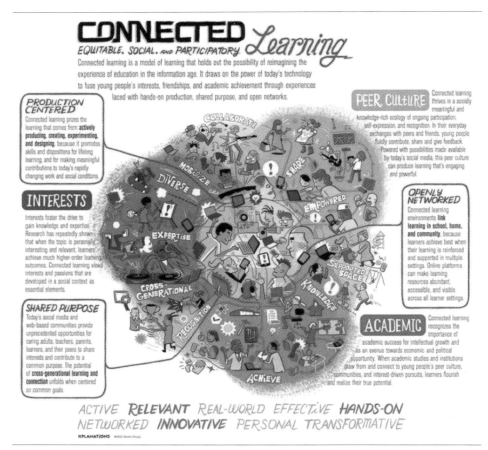

Thus, the Connected Learning Framework (Ito et al., 2013) suggests that

connected learning is realized when a young person pursues a personal interest or passion with the support of friends and caring adults, and is in turn able to link this learning and interest to academic achievement, career possibilities, or civic engagement.
Digital and networked media offer new ways of expanding the reach and accessibility
of connected learning so it is not just privileged youth who have these opportunities.
Connected learning looks to digital media and communications to: 1) offer engaging
formats for interactivity and self-expression, 2) lower barriers to access for knowledge
and information, 3) provide social supports for learning through social media and
online affinity groups, and 4) link a broader and more diverse range of culture, knowledge, and expertise to educational opportunity. (p. 6)

Theoretical Influence: Connected Learning

Context	Core properties
• Peer supported	• Production centered
• Interest powered	• Shared purpose
• Academically oriented	• Openly networked
Design principles	**Use of new media**
• Everyone participates	• Engagement and self-expression
• Learning by doing	• Accessibility
• Constant challenge (flow)	• Social support
• Interconnected	• Diversity and capacity

Just as Ito et al. argue for the positive applications of digital media and communications, we too contend that such media can contribute to the rich, multifaceted reading lives of adolescents. Connected Reading takes into account that "engaging formats" and "social supports" are key elements for digital readers.

Contextual Factors and Reader Attributes

In her seminal work, *The Reader, the Text, the Poem: The Transactional Theory of the Literary Work*, Rosenblatt (1978) describes an interaction between "the reader" and "the text" to create an interpretation, or "the poem." This interpretation is unique for each individual, as every reader brings personal knowledge and beliefs to the individualized contexts of his or her reading. Rosenblatt also argues that reading can be aesthetic (for pleasure) or efferent (for meaning), and her theory has influenced a generation of scholars and teachers who consider the purposes of reading in school.

For instance, Gallagher (2009) provocatively titled one of his recent books *Readicide: How Schools Are Killing Reading and What You Can Do about It*. Other authors, such as Smith and Wilhelm (2002, 2006; Wilhelm & Smith, 2014), also have been concerned about how we, in school, can unintentionally suck the joy out of reading. Moreover, Miller (2009) has become known for her work as "the book whisperer," and Kittle (2013) recently founded the Book Love Foundation. Teachers and scholars in our field have worked to preserve the aesthetic foundation of reading articulated by Rosenblatt.

Therefore, any discussion about adolescent reading practices, as well as instructional approaches to teaching reading in middle or high school, must acknowledge the role of self-selected, interest-driven reading. While teens are likely to embrace some canonical and contemporary texts that we want or need to teach as part of our curriculum, they are also likely to engage in many, many hours of self-sponsored reading, oftentimes sharing their ideas about those texts with friends. As Wilhelm & Smith, (2014) note,

> while neglecting their homework, even the most reluctant of these students would be reading. Astonishingly, some read 600, 700, even 800 minutes a week. These supposed non-readers would sometimes form friendship groups around their free-choice reading, talking passionately together about authors and trading books and ideas. (p. 15)

When teens read what interests them, they connect readily with other readers who share their interests. More and more, they find these texts and make these connections through digital devices. Both the context and the specific attributes of the reader, including vocabulary knowledge, fluency, and all of those characteristics noted by Rosenblatt, influence the reader's initial encounter and ongoing engagement with a text.

Given the interaction between reader and text in Rosenblatt's theory, our model of Connected Reading suggests that Rosenblatt's ideas are extremely important in understanding comprehension in a digital world. First, we argue that in addition to the reader and the text, we must also consider the role of devices in the transaction. Though it may not matter in terms of the *content* where an individual reads Shakespeare, we need to understand that the device itself (print book,

Theoretical Influence: Importance of Reader in Transaction

Contextual Factors	Individual Reader Attributes
• School-based vs. self-selected reading tasks	• Interest and motivation, including previous experiences with reading in general, specific genres and authors, as well as reading instruction
• Print, digital, or multiple formats for reading (multimedia, audiobooks)	• Fluency, including automaticity (understanding words quickly and independently) and prosody (patterns of pronunciation and emphasis)
• Reading done in place, typically as a lesson or during silent reading time, or reading that is happening on-the-go, typically with mobile devices	• Vocabulary (both working, receptive vocabulary as well as specific academic, disciplinary vocabulary)

computer, tablet, handheld) may shape the *interaction* because it changes the form of the text and/or it offers tools that allow a reader to engage in different ways (e.g., using a dictionary).

More important, however, as we noted earlier, hypertext presents text features that do not simply invite a reader into the text; rather, hypertext demands reader participation. Though Rosenblatt suggests that texts do not live without a reader, for networked texts the reader must create the text itself by following links. There are seemingly infinite numbers of textual constructions, depending on the path of any given reader. In a hyperlinked arena, a transaction between reader and text is physically visible in the creation of the text itself. Because it would not make sense to read these kinds of texts on a printed page, devices (and choices surrounding their use) become an important part of the transaction.

Connected Reading, Not Just Digital Reading

Connected Reading positions readers as active participants in broader communities of practice, communities that are driven by authentic purposes and academically engaging work. While we understand that some readers may have a greater affinity for personal reading, some for school reading, and some may want more reading in their lives and some less, we also recognize that we are responsible for teaching them *all* to read. This goal blends issues of equity and access to texts, differentiation and scaffolding for learners of different capabilities, and a balance between self-selected and curricular decisions.

In other words, we recognize the diversity of readers in our world, especially adolescent readers. Although we suggest that this diversity is growing in a digital age, we do not see Connected Reading as limited to reading of just digital texts. We live in an era when readers navigate across devices, as well as across print and digital forms. Connected Reading embraces all kinds of reading, noting how textual features and contexts that include digital or print devices may shape a reading experience. Therefore, in this book we share examples of both print and digital texts. But we understand that reading of print texts has a long and rich history from which teachers can draw for their practice. Our focus is on articulating how digital texts might be different—and how we can develop Connected Readers in our classrooms using digital tools, regardless of the type of text available.

With this focus on digital texts, we are left with a number of questions: What dispositions do our students bring to the Internet? How do they encounter, engage with, and evaluate texts? What exactly do these practices look like for different readers? How does making reading more visibly social affect what students know and are able to do?

In an era when e-readers, mobile devices, and Web-based texts represent a major portion of our daily reading material, teachers cannot ignore how these tools and texts fit into reading instruction. As teachers, we must assume that adolescents are reading digitally outside of school, and therefore it is vital that we prepare them to read these texts critically and mindfully. With this premise in mind, we now turn our attention to putting the ideas behind Connected Reading into practice.

Connected Reading in Practice

Reading each morning starts for me, as for many other professionals, with what I hope will be just a quick glance at my email. Skimming the additions to my inbox, I make sure there are no issues that need my immediate, personal attention. Then I move on to the second tier of messages that include announcements, email newsletters, listserv responses, and other personal correspondence. Despite my efforts to reduce spam and clutter, there are still many items that must simply be deleted. Shifting my attention, I look carefully at some of the headlines from NCTE's INBOX, Edutopia's newsletter, and a daily summary of education news, clicking on one or two articles to read them more carefully. Of course, messages that require a response stay in my inbox; everything else is archived. Once I have made my inbox manageable using this utilitarian set of reading skills, I move on with my morning, knowing exactly what messages I can read again and respond to later.

Remember that all links and handouts are located on the companion wiki. Scan this QR code or go to http://connectedreading.wikispaces.com to access Chapter 3 materials.

Throughout this chapter, by way of these brief interludes, we share glimpses of our own reading practices, as well as those of two of the students we interviewed. In our reflections, we have tried to document both what we read as well as reasons for why and how we read and, in the spirit of the larger argument we are making in this book, how we share our reading. We offer these anecdotes to show Connected Reading practices in action, and we invite you to think about your reading, too, through the use of sidebar questions embedded throughout the chapter.

While choices about what and how to read have always been mediated by time, space, and access, your choices as a reader have become more numerous in a digital age. Sometimes the reason for a choice in the medium of text is simple: it is available only in digital or in print form. Other times a reader makes a conscious choice between digital and physical text. For instance, a copy of *English Journal* arrives in the mail, but for Troy it is more useful to download the journal on his iPad because he can then carry it—as well as about half a dozen other articles—as a digital copy to be read at convenient times. Kristen, on the other hand, grabs the paper version for her train ride because it is lighter than her iPad in her already heavy commuter bag.

Questions about what, how, and when to read dominate our lives. Do I buy that new book and have it shipped in two days? Or do I download it now? Or do I get on the waiting list at the library? Is this news story worth a deep reading now, or do I tag it and come back later? And though we admit that not everyone begins the day as Troy does, curating email and digital headlines, our strong hunch is that you (and your students) do cross boundaries between print and digital text many times and throughout the day.

Kristen's father-in-law, for instance, recently described to her his mixed reading practices. In the car, he listens to an audio version of a book; at home he picks up where the audio left off by reading a print version. By the end of the book, he has traversed both media to draw meaning from the text, and he can't discern from which media he "read" which parts of the book. We know he is not alone in his ability to navigate multiple forms of text or in his desire to do so (and that companies such as Amazon and Audible have now teamed up to make the transition from reading to listening automatic), and we hope you will take this opportunity to consider how you (and your students) have developed the ability and inclination to read many kinds of texts.

Once my family's morning routines are underway, I also peek at my Twitter notifications to see if there is anything I should be reading, though I don't have a ton of time to spend reading while hustling kids to get ready for school. Before I leave the house, however, it is likely that I will spend at least another few minutes looking through the headlines that have come in via my RSS reader of choice, Feedly. Long gone are the days of walking out to the mailbox in the morning to retrieve a paper. Instead, the headlines from our local paper—owned by an international conglomerate—as well as various other news sources, bloggers, and Google alerts that I have set up all come to my Feedly account.

Knowing that at certain sites I can read only a few of the stories each month that are available in front of the pay-wall, I choose wisely from the major news sources. Also, I look to see what other colleagues have posted to their blogs, especially items related to technology and writing. My Google Alerts for "technology and education" as well as "writing and education" round out my Feedly reading list. I see that, as with my email, I have many unread feeds. Like that nagging inbox, I see dozens or even hundreds of unread stories, but I have to make choices about what to read each day, so I simply let these go.

What We Read: Digital Text Types

I have grown as a digital reader over the last few years, but I yearn to be fluid in my curating, annotating, and archiving of texts. More often than not, I am overwhelmed by the amount of information that comes across my desk. With hundreds of emails in my personal and professional inboxes (I play many roles in life and so have many accounts that align with those roles), stacks of both virtual and paper articles, and pages and pages of student writing to be read, I find little time to manage social networks and RSS feeds. Though I have a Twitter account where I have curated a personal learning network, I read it sparingly, focusing my attention mostly on Facebook, where I connect with professional colleagues, friends, and family. Once or twice a day, I scan my news feed and click on articles that interest me, opening them in new tabs on my Internet browser so I can read them at a convenient time. Sometimes I read ebooks on my iPad, often bingeing by downloading three or four at a time from my local public library. More often than not, however, I have a stack of unfinished paperbacks on my nightstand. For me, the choice is not a preference of digital or print; it is a matter of time and energy for reading and what I have available to me in the moment.

Kristen's reading practices reflect those of many people who feel tugged in different directions and overwhelmed by the possibilities of the Internet for providing texts across devices and platforms. In contrast to Trevor (Figure 3.1), who describes distractions as a form of entertainment—and we agree that reading can and should sometimes be leisurely and for pleasure—Kristen is distracted by competing priorities, most often for professional purposes. From the latest social network posts to related links on a Web-based article, readers never lack for a variety of digital texts from which to choose. But how do we read those texts? What textual features influence our choices and processes?

Figure 3.1. A profile of Trevor as a reader.

Trevor, a sophomore, likes comics, mysteries, and the Diary of a Wimpy Kid series. He has read several of the books in that series. Reading a novel can be pleasurable for him, yet he says that "I'm not that big of a reader, but I like novels here and there. Only certain novels grab my attention." Instead,

> I'd rather read on the computer, but in a way, I'd rather read in a book because the computer can distract you. But it's more like, it's like a feeling that you have when you read it on a computer more than with a book. Like when you're reading it in a book, it's kind of dead, like you really don't feel everything as much as [on] the computer.

Even though he enjoys this type of reading, Trevor recognizes that he can become distracted on a computer: "Sometimes I get off-task. If I see like an ad or something, I'll click on the ad, or I want to go on Facebook or websites. And like it gets me distracted from what I'm supposed to be doing."

Trevor manages this distraction in a few ways. One strategy is to start with homework, or as he says, "Homework first and then you could have fun or whatever." When possible, he reads homework assignments on the iPad because "you can't multitask with the iPad; . . . you're forced to stay on-task because if you have to exit out . . . sometimes it will close the page and you will lose everything." He also uses a "parent app" to keep himself locked in his assigned task. Though distraction is a constant struggle, he says, "I'm getting better and better at staying on-task."

After he completes his homework, Trevor is free to read what interests him, including articles about newly released games, strategies for game play, and the news. He reads news articles two to three times a week so that he can "know what's happening around my surroundings." He finds these articles serendipitously on his Yahoo homepage or through purposeful searches. Sometimes he does these searches based on stories he hears in his Global History class. As he says, "I take it a step further to see for myself what happened."

Like many teens, Trevor uses Facebook, the only social network to which he belongs. He scrolls through his news feed and will read further if "it's someone that's very important to me. . . . [T]hen I'll read it so I can be more involved with them and help them." Sometimes he will use Google to further research a comment on Facebook "so I find the information for myself." These three avenues—Facebook, Yahoo, and purposeful searching based on face-to-face conversations—lead him to much of his out-of-school reading.

Though he admits that books help him to be less distracted, and he does read novels in print form, Trevor would rather read on a tablet or computer because "those things bring me entertainment." Like all readers, especially those of us now using digital devices, Trevor balances a variety of choices and priorities, pursuing topics of academic and personal interest while also struggling with distractions that are meant primarily for pleasure.

Each of these glimpses into a reading life—Troy's, Kristen's, and Trevor's—highlights a number of the questions we face about when, where, and how to read. We have developed a set of questions in the sidebar that you can use to explore your own reading life. As we move forward in this chapter, we are specifically interested in the kinds of reading that come in the form of digital texts, either because these readings are born-digital texts (e.g., websites, interactive ebooks) or because it is more convenient for us to read them as digital texts (e.g., a newspaper article or basic ebook). To explore these ideas further, we first identify and then think through the affordances and constraints offered by various forms of digital texts.

In their chapter "The Changing Landscape of Text and Comprehension in the Age of New Literacies," Dalton and Proctor (2008) articulate four varieties of "digital texts," a set of distinctions that are useful for us to consider as we think about the kinds of texts we and our students encounter each day. They describe the following:

- "linear text in digital format," such as a novel downloaded from Project Gutenberg or purchased from Amazon
- "non linear text with hyperlinks," such as a webpage with links to various other sources
- "text with integrated media," such as a webpage with audio and video clips or an interactive map
- "text with response options," such as a discussion forum or invitation to email the author (300)

We recognize that these forms do not neatly map on to definitions of all types of digital texts. For instance, we wonder: is an entire website considered linear, because pages have an organizational structure and can be read alone, or nonlinear, because any one page on a site may have internal and external links that a reader can follow? Still, we think that these broad categories are useful. Dalton and Proctor argue, and we agree, that all forms of digital text offer readers a variety of new options for comprehension. Still, they cautiously claim that

---

Thinking through Text Types

- What kinds of texts do you read (news stories, novels, emails, websites, magazines)?

- How have you organized your reading across the various roles you play in your personal and professional life?

- At what point, when a text is available in both formats, do you make a conscious choice between print and digital text?

- How do you choose the device you will use to read?

- What factors figure into how you make all these choices?

in order for the role of the text to be expanded as we suggest, learners must avail themselves of the affordances offered. This is not a simple matter, given the evolving nature of digital tools and texts and the complexity of new literacies. (320)

Indeed, consideration of the "affordances offered" by digital texts—affordances such as links to outside resources, embedded audio and video, or other supplementary materials not offered in print—is incredibly important, and throughout this book, we argue that mindfulness plays a key role in the comprehension of digital texts.

We explore the first three of Dalton and Proctor's (2008) types of texts in turn. However, because nearly all digital texts now offer some kind of response option via commenting, by communicating with the author, or by posting to social networks, we integrate our discussion of the fourth type, "text with response options," recognizing that in the current landscape of digital tools and digital texts, reading and response are a recursive, nearly simultaneous process. For each of the three types—linear text in digital format, nonlinear text with hyperlinks, and fully integrated multimedia text—we describe what they look like and offer examples, documenting the response that may occur when readers engage with them.

Linear Text in Digital Format

Trevor, who is profiled in Figure 3.1, seems to draw a clear line between print and digital texts. For him "novels" are print and everything else is digital. During his interview, he never suggested that a book might come in digital form. Sienna (Figure 3.2), on the other hand, understands that with the introduction of e-readers and tablets, books can in fact be digital, and a linear text in digital format is a close cousin to a traditional novel. In other words, a linear text in digital format acts like the print books that both Sienna and Trevor describe—the books we know and love—but without the comfort of a cover and binding, or the smell of paper and ink.

For instance, we may be able to read the actual text of a classic work of literature that is available in the public domain, say *The Adventures of Tom Sawyer*, as a linear text in digital format because it is available through the Project Gutenberg website, Apple's iBooks store, or, as Sienna notes, in the free Kindle library. We can download a copy, open it on our tablet or dedicated e-reader device, and then the text itself behaves very much like a book. There are no embedded links, though there may be some navigational and interactive features, such as links to chapters, dictionaries, and highlighting, that are available in this basic ebook format. The text, rather than appearing on paper, simply appears on screen instead.

Because these kinds of texts are meant to be read in a linear fashion, they align with our expectations of what typical books offer: one story, from beginning to end. Still, we return to the arguments on text complexity and close reading that

Figure 3.2. A profile of Sienna as a reader.

Sienna, a ninth grader, got a Kindle for Christmas a year ago, and though she didn't use it at first, once she found out that she could access a free library of books, it became her primary reading tool. She borrows a lot of books online, but she buys her favorites in print copy because, as she says, "I just like to have those around and read them because they're like old friends and they kind of show . . . different areas where you were when you were growing up." She likes to read "epic novels" and "deep philosophical things," and she says, "I think it's important to read stories. . . . It's a good way to think."

She likes to read series of books "that have a bit of a following . . . because you can find common ground with people." One series she has read is Harry Potter, and she has even read on Pottermore, a website that provides background on the books and authorial choices, and she uses this reading to "apply [her] knowledge . . . as another layer" to the novels.

Though Sienna traverses media easily, she understands a difference between her print and digital reading—and the affordances of each. For instance, she describes the difference between browsing on a Kindle and in the public library:

When I have a specific book, series, or author in mind, it is a lot easier for me to use a digital library because I can just type in the keywords and find it. But when I don't have anything particular in mind and I want to browse, I greatly prefer the physical library because you can just walk along the shelves and look at whatever catches your eye. One time during the summer I went back to the library and I just looked through all the books and wrote down all the names of the books that I wanted to read. And that's cool because it leads you to look at stuff that you might not have actually read, whereas if you're browsing [digitally] and you went to look by genre then you tend to be confined to a certain thing. And that gets monotonous.

Once she finds a text to read, either digitally or in print, Sienna will often download it on her Kindle, which she says is a "really good way to read more challenging stuff" because of the built-in dictionary feature. "Right now I'm reading *Brave New World* in the actual book form, and I found that there's a lot of words that I don't understand because they might be more medical terms, and so I've been writing them down, but it's easier when you can get the instant gratification of looking it up [in a digital version of the book]."

Sienna says she has a hard time keeping up with social media and doesn't use it a lot, but she uses email with her friends, and "I often share links to stuff about recent music and books." As she says, "If I see a post on something and I'm like whoa, this is really cool; I have not heard about this. Thank you, this website, for showing me this, and then if I really like it, I will forward it to my friends."

Sienna will click on headlines occasionally but she will also read the paper copy of the newspaper, which is how she keeps informed. However, she notes the benefits of online reading: "Online, you don't have the confines of actual physical space. So you can put as much information as you want on and you can find more information about articles." If she is interested in a topic, she will search for it using Google.

Sienna is familiar with transmedia stories, too. She encountered them on YouTube, where she learned of an "adaptation of Jane Austen novels into a modern day blog format and . . . social media to keep updates." She says the story is "really cool" and that it inspired her to read *Pride and Prejudice*.

Moving back and forth across reading genres and platforms, Sienna is an adept reader who makes intentional choices about what, when, and how to read. She recognizes the advantages and disadvantages of reading and interacting with various forms of text and seems to have found a balance that works for her as a highly motivated reader.

are presented in the NCTE policy brief: Lexile scores are only one measure of the text's complexity, and close reading by itself cannot guarantee that students deeply engage with the text. As we describe in Chapter 6, digital features can be employed in strategic ways as readers make their way through texts, supporting comprehension and meaning making. Thus, even though not much more than a regular book or article taken from page and put on-screen, linear text in digital format offers limited yet useful opportunities to interact with texts.

My family has always connected through reading. My mom, dad, brother, and I began initialing the front covers of books after we read so that we knew who to pass the book to next. When I first began dating my husband, I stood in front of his father's bookshelf and, realizing we had similar tastes, we too started sharing books. We talked about our reading and passed titles, as well as physical books, back and forth. Recently, he commented on a novel that he wanted to read, and I responded that I had read it via ebook. This marked a turn in our reading lives: because the novel did not sit on my nightstand, I forgot to mention it to him; because it was not a hard copy, I could not share it. I have noticed a similar shift in practice among my nuclear family, especially my dad and brother, who read digitally on e-readers on a regular basis. We share texts less often. My social network, however, shares more frequently. Lynne posts reviews on Goodreads that come to my feed; Heather asks for reading recommendations before her trip to the beach, and she gets a flurry of replies that fuel my own reading list; Mark comments on the newest YA book he has read and shares a list of top reads. These response options work for both print and digital texts, and they connect us as readers across time and space, just as my family has always connected.

Thinking through How to Find Books

- In what ways do you find books to read? In what ways do your students find books?

- How do you share your thoughts and ideas from those books? How do your students share?

- What is gained and what is lost for you when browsing books in digital form as compared to print form?

- Have you used Amazon, Google Books, or another source to preview a book before borrowing it from the library or purchasing it in print or digital form?

As Kristen's experience demonstrates, response and sharing have been a part of the process for engaged readers since long before television book clubs popularized them. We've each heard some version of the old adage that "a reader is never done with a book until it is shared." From reviews on Amazon or other booksellers' websites to the types of personal recommendations that Kristen describes coming through the Facebook feed, we are finding more and more ways to use digital tools as a means of sharing our linear reading experiences.

Nonlinear Text with Hyperlinks

In contrast to a linear text in digital format, we should expect a nonlinear text with hyperlinks to be a text that is specifically designed for reading in a computer-mediated environment. In fact, it has to be read that way—on-screen and with links as a hypertext—to fully appreciate it. While we may be able to enjoy a work of hypertext fiction after printing out every single page and assembling them into one document, this is not the purpose of hypertext. Hypertext provides readers and writers with the opportunity to collaborate in the meaning-making process, clicking forward and backward on links. This interactivity becomes a defining characteristic of hypertext, and perhaps without our realizing it, we associate hypertext reading with digital reading. Trevor certainly does as he describes the differences between the "effects" of books and reading on the iPad or computer. For him, and for many of us, nonlinear texts with hyperlinks can lead to distractions, and we must consider the strategies we use to comprehend such texts.

There have been many versions of hypertext over the years, and one of the first professional books for English teachers to explore connections between hypertext and the English classroom is Wilhelm and Friedemann's *Hyperlearning: Where Projects, Inquiry, and Technology Meet* (1998). They argue:

> We believe that to be literate in the twenty-first century, students must become composers and readers of hypermedia. They must understand its possibilities, uses, and design. Since our future texts, even more so than our current ones, will be hypertextual, students will need to understand the conventions and construction of such texts. (p. 20)

While some hypertext theorists might quibble with the intersecting use of terms such as *hypermedia* and *hypertext*, Wilhelm and colleagues made the case for teaching the "conventions and construction" of hypertext nearly two decades ago, and it is a type of text that many of us still struggle to implement in our reading instruction. To what extent do we provide our students with specific opportunities to truly read and comprehend hypertextual documents? To what extent do we model that process for them? How do we engage all readers in these kinds of texts? How do we help students like Trevor learn to stay focused in a sea

Thinking through Hypertext

- When did you first read a nonlinear text? Perhaps it was a Choose Your Own Adventure book in childhood. Perhaps it was a website. What do you remember about this experience?

- How has hypertext changed the manner in which you read? Do you, like Trevor, get distracted when reading online? What techniques do you use to keep yourself focused?

- Have you engaged fully in a work of hypertext fiction or nonfiction? Or are you more apt to read individual articles and webpages that link to yet more pages, though not as an intentionally "whole" text?

- How do you talk about hypertext reading with your students? What strategies do you employ? What have they suggested to you?

of distractions? How do we help students like Sienna understand and appreciate hypertext fiction in the same way that they enjoy a regular novel?

Reading Instruction for All *Students* acknowledges that these kinds of digital texts are different. Status updates contain links to articles that contain links to even more articles. Wikipedia is filled with internal references inside its articles, as well as outside resources listed at the end of each article. Bloggers and journalists might include a link as both a de facto citation and a rhetorical move in writing. And anyone who has clicked on something that appeared to be legitimate but turns out to be an ad knows that some links are, indeed, more nefarious than others. We must consider how to teach adolescents to choose and interact mindfully with nonlinear texts with hyperlinks. If we do not, they may get lost, as we like to say, "down the rabbit hole."

In short, hypertext exists across many reading spaces, and its uses are nearly endless, as Kristen shares here.

As much as I enjoy losing myself in a book, hypertext dominates my reading life. I follow links on social networks, and I dig down into the links of the articles that I find. I share important links myself on these same networks. I subscribe to various blogs and receive their posts via RSS and email, and when I am really interested in what the author has said, I dig down into the links they provide. I often respond via the comment tool on the original post, sharing my own interpretation or experience. I receive and share links with my colleagues and family, and I dig down to investigate the validity of the claims. When appropriate, I engage in conversation about the texts, both virtually and in person. The ability to immediately and easily dig down and to instantaneously respond is part of the beauty of hypertext.

As with the linear texts she described earlier, Kristen demonstrates the ways in which she shares and responds to various forms of hypertext. Again, it is difficult to separate the idea of "reading" from that of "writing" or "response" because these activities work in parallel with one another. Kristen's ability to interrogate a particular text by following links, offering commentary, and sharing new links with her social networks demonstrates just three ways in which hypertext has changed her reading experience to one of immediate relevance. The ability to quickly access a text via hyperlink, as well as additional related texts from more links, makes this form of reading particularly powerful when pursuing new topics and ideas.

A Text with Integrated Media

As tablets and e-readers have caught up with the capabilities of the Web, we now have access to ebooks and magazines that have the same types of interactive features as websites. Rather than simply being used as a technological enhancement, audio and video that are truly integrated into a text are crucial to the story itself, and readers need to engage with this multimedia to understand the story.

Sienna describes one example of a multimedia text: a transmedia story based on the novels of Jane Austen that uses video, blogs, and social media to move the action. Another example, *Inanimate Alice* (www.inanimatealice.com/), is described on the site as "a reading-from-the-screen experience for the digital generation" that "uses text, images, music, sound effects, puzzles and games to illustrate and enhance the narrative" ("About" section). Like a book, *Inanimate Alice* has chapters that the reader progresses through, each revealing more about Alice and her family. Fleming (2013), a high school library and media specialist, describes the combination of media in this way:

> The interactivity and narrative are not distinct from one another. In the case of *Inanimate Alice*, the interactive elements simply cannot be separated from the story. Whether it is controlling Alice's Baxi (her handheld gaming device) or communicating with Brad (her virtual friend on the Baxi), the embedded technology enhances the narrative and helps it to unfold in manifold directions under the reader's impulse. It is this that makes Alice a truly unique digital reading experience. (p. 374)

Texts with integrated media can also come as long-form journalism. For instance, the *New York Times* piece "Snow Fall: The Avalanche at Tunnel Creek" (Branch, 2012) won a Pulitzer in 2013, and many news pieces now include short video clips along with alphabetic text as well. When arriving on the "Snow Fall" website, viewers are greeted with an image that shows snow blowing across the ground, and the title fades in. Then, scrolling down, readers encounter the text of the article, including certain sentences that are lightly highlighted, with a video icon next to them. Clicking on that sentence will play a video embedded next to the paragraph. Other features of the online story include a map, archival figures, slideshows, and links to additional pages in the story. Reading the "Snow Fall" story is inherently a multimodal, interactive experience.

Like these Web-based reading experiences, Larson (2009) explains the potential for the interactive features of ebooks:

> Many e-books employ multimodal features—such as video, audio, and hyperlinks—as well as interactive tools. Such tools invite readers to physically interact with the text

through inserting, deleting, or replacing text; marking passages by highlighting, underlining, or crossing out words; adding comments by inserting notes, attaching files, or recording audio comments; and manipulating the page format, text size, and screen layout. (p. 255)

Whether in ebook form or embedded in a website, these features create new challenges for readers. We have long understood the text features that constitute well-structured texts, especially in nonfiction. Headings, captions, graphics, bold print: all of these text features have the potential to contribute to a reader's ability to make meaning. Will interactive ebooks or immersive websites rely on similar features, or will new ones emerge? Gamers have long searched for hidden "Easter eggs" in their quests in order to find extended narratives, additional characters, and other rewards, and now interactive ebooks and transmedia stories often employ similar techniques. How do we manage our reading experience when we are moving across various forms of media and when navigating those various forms is crucial to our overall understanding of the text?

Texts with integrated media are, as Fleming (2013) states, "truly unique," yet the popularity of such texts is growing, and educators see value in them for learning. NCTE recently published its first multimedia text (Gere, Homan, Parsons, Spooner, & Uzogara, 2014), and we suspect it will not be the last.

The preface of *Text Complexity: Supporting Student Readers* [NCTE, 2014] invited me to read the book "from beginning to end" or "in bits and snatches." Typically when I read professional texts, I skim the entire book before going back to focus in on particular chapters, so I immediately thought that I would be a "beginning to end" reader of this ebook. Four pages into Chapter 1, I clicked a link—and I knew my reading of this text would be different. As I moved through the book, I found myself watching teacher reflections presented in video form. I accepted the authors' invitation to take notes in my e-reader on my own reading of a passage—and I clicked through to the appendix, where I could compare my notes to author reflections. I snapped a picture and sent it to Troy with my notes. I jumped around, reading in "bits and snatches" and interacting with the text and its multimedia components in my own meaningful path.

It is these texts with integrated media options that provide us with the most excitement as we think about the future of reading instruction yet at the same time cause us the most concern when we consider the implementation of CCSS. The NCTE policy statement suggests that teachers ask students to consider the unique features of these kinds of texts, and indeed we must also ask students to reflect on how they engage with these features to make meaning. In fact, the multimedia components constitute a significant portion of the meaning-making process. Without them, the text would not be complete.

Whether a linear text in a digital format, a nonlinear text with hyperlinks, or a text with media integrated throughout—and whether presented as an ebook, a website, or an app—we must acknowledge the changing shape of texts that our students encounter inside and outside of school.

Thinking through Multimedia

- Have you read a text that has multimedia embedded? Did you feel that the multimedia was a critical component of the text, helping you make meaning of the whole?

- How is your reading of this type of text different from reading linear texts? What do you focus on first? Text? Media? Why?

- As we invite students to read, view, and participate with these types of multimedia texts, what skills will they need to bring as readers, listeners, and viewers?

Where We Read: Apps and Web

Throughout the day, I scan my email, not just to put out fires, but to see if any new links have come in. Fortunately, the recent update to my Gmail app makes this task even easier because of the tabs it creates for my primary inbox as well as "Social," "Updates," and "Forums" sections. This top-level organization allows me to skim the total number of emails I have and decide if I want to dive in to any particular one for more information.

At other points, I will employ two different apps to keep up on my current professional reading from the "Edublogosphere" and "Twitterverse." First, I use the RSS aggregator Feedly, which allows me to quickly skim and scan many news sources, blogs, and custom Google Alerts that I have set up for myself, including ones on "education and writing" as well as "education and technology." Because of Feedly's layout, I am not able to read the entire article at once, at least not easily, and sometimes I will click an ellipsis icon to select a way to share an article. I can send it to Pocket, a separate app that will allow me to read the entire article later, even if I am offline. Or I can send the article via email, often to myself so I remember to click on it later.

My other main reading app, Flipboard, functions like a virtual magazine. By connecting my Facebook and Twitter accounts, as well as selecting from many existing Flipboard magazines and custom search terms, I am able to see a number of headlines, introductions to articles, and, if included in the original piece online, a representative photo. Flipboard, as its name implies, allows me to flip through pages, much like reading a newspaper or magazine. Unlike those print sources, Flipboard is constantly updating. Rather than looking at a list of headlines, as with Feedly, or a series of links, as on Twitter, Flipboard allows me to get a much better sense of what I am about to read. Along with sections such as "*NPR,*" "*The Atlantic,*" and "*The Daily Beast,*" I also delve into the latest tech news, the #engchat Twitter stream, and, just for fun, "*The Onion*" and "*I Can Has Cheezburger?*" If I find something I want to read in more detail, I will save it to Pocket or send it to email.

These apps keep me organized as my reading life spans multiple websites and social networks, allowing me to move effortlessly from one reading experience to the next.

In this section, we differentiate between two types of digital reading, each powered in the same manner: reading on the Web and reading with applications, known more widely as apps. Interestingly enough, the actual text we read, albeit in digital form, is the same. When Extensible Markup Language (XML) and Cascading Style Sheets (CSS) became the new standards for webpage design in the early 2000s, hypertext as we knew it went through a separation of content and form. While neither of us is a computer programmer or has intricate knowledge of how all of this works, we have been informed by the work of cultural anthropologist Michael Wesch and his intriguing video, "The Machine Is Us/Using Us (final version)" (2007), which we strongly encourage you to view before you consider the implications of Web-based text on your students' reading.

In short, XML, CSS, and the opportunities created by Web browsers and mobile devices for content delivery provide us with a new set of reading opportunities, even if we are looking at the same actual text. For instance, when Troy loads Feedly on his phone, he sees a preview of a new blog post, which he may choose to save to Pocket. Later, when he has more time to read, he logs on to his Pocket account in a Web browser, where he finds the same text in a different form. Content can be delivered anywhere; form—including fonts, color schemes, and other readability functions—can be adjusted based on the device being used. Because content is separated from form, we are able to view text in a variety of ways.

As an example, look at how one of Troy's recent blog posts appears across a variety of platforms (Figure 3.3). First is a screenshot as viewed through a Web browser on a computer, and this represents a fairly standard view of a typical blog, complete with formatting and additional widgets placed there by the blogger (Figure 3.3a).

Next is the same text from Troy's blog, though he has activated Evernote's Clearly tool, which, as described on the company's website, "makes blog posts, articles and webpages clean and easy to read" (Figure 3.3b). While Troy works hard to keep ads off his site, we have all experienced websites with extreme amounts of clutter, and Clearly, quite simply, wipes away all the clutter to make the reading experience very much like looking at a single article on paper.

Figure 3.3. Screenshots of the same blog post in multiple reading platforms.

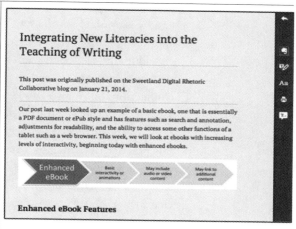

a. Troy's blog post as viewed in a typical Web browser.

b. Troy's blog post as viewed in a Web browser with Evernote's Clearly extension enabled.

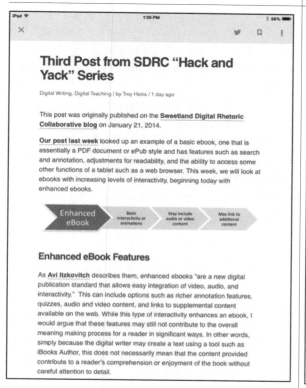

c. Troy's blog post as viewed in the Feedly app for iPad.

d. Troy's blog post as viewed in the Pocket app for iPad.

Third, we look at this same blog post through the lens of Feedly, an RSS reader that allows you to subscribe to the news feeds coming from many websites, blogs, and other forms of media such as videos, podcasts, and photos (Figure 3.3c). Feedly is available both as a website, viewable in any Web browser, as well as an app for use on smartphones and tablets.

Finally, we see the same blog post as it is saved to Pocket (Figure 3.3d). Pocket allows you to read the article in full at a later time, even without an Internet connection, but it also allows you to go online to read the original material in Web form if you do have an Internet connection.

Even for those of us accustomed to reading digital text across many devices, this practice of managing when, where, and how to read a digital text can be overwhelming at first. Some apps work across browsers, devices, and platforms. Others require a particular browser such as Firefox or Google Chrome, or a particular device such as an iOS or Android operating system. But once you are able to swiftly manage your reading experiences with these tools, they can become invaluable as a part of your daily reading habit, allowing deeper engagement with many texts.

As we think about just this batch of digital reading tools, we must consider a few teaching points. First, digital text is malleable and can come to us in a variety of forms. Helping students understand which websites and apps are most useful for them as individual readers requires that we, as adult readers, become at least passingly familiar with the options afforded by each. This does not mean that you as teacher must become expert in each and every one of these technologies. Having a basic understanding of how each one works is essential, however, and we capture some of those features in Figure 3.4. Second, and more important, we need to be even more vigilant in our efforts to help students find a variety of perspectives on their topics. This includes perspectives from mass media, the scientific community, and individual bloggers, as well as from both ends of the political spectrum. The tools may bring us new items to read, yet critical thinking is even more important now as our sources continue to multiply.

Figure 3.4. Apps for digital reading.

Evernote's Clearly http://evernote.com/clearly As an extension of the popular organizational tool Evernote, Clearly takes away the clutter from webpages, making the articles themselves the main focus without advertisements, sidebars, and other distractions. This browser extension is available for Google Chrome, Firefox, and Opera. Safari has a similar feature with its "Reader" function that will show up in the URL bar for any website that can be read in this mode. 	**Flipboard** http://flipboard.com As an app designed for mobile devices, Flipboard describes itself as a "magazine." In this sense, a reader is able to open up the app and quickly browse through different sections; these sections can be prepopulated by Flipboard, or users can curate their own sections by adding various news sources, blogs, or other RSS feeds. Recently, Flipboard added functionality to take items found on the Web through normal browsing, and then press a button to "Flip it" into your own custom magazine. Flipboard is now available for iOS, Android, Windows, and BlackBerry. Flipboard also allows you to quickly share items via email or social networks.
Other options like Clearly to reduce screen clutter: Readability (cross platform) Enjoy Reading (Firefox only) Purify (Google Chrome only)	Other options like Flipboard: Pulse (iOS, Android) News360 (iOS, Android, Windows) Zite (iOS, Android, Windows) Google Currents (iOS, Android)
Feedly http://feedly.com/i/welcome With the demise of Google Reader in 2013, a number of RSS tools looked to fill its place. Feedly immediately rose to the top of many bloggers' lists as an alternative. With the ability to read RSS feeds through a browser or using the Feedly app (iOS, Android, Kindle Fire, Windows), you can keep up with a wide variety of news sources as easily as you skim your email. Feedly allows for quick views of individual stories and the ability to easily share these stories across social networks and other reading apps. The unique ability to read via browser or mobile app makes Feedly and other tools like it especially useful.	**Pocket** https://getpocket.com Like Feedly, Pocket is a tool that works across multiple devices and platforms. Allowing the user to bookmark content through a browser, Pocket then loads up a reading list for later that can be accessed online or off. With extensions for Firefox and Chrome, as well as apps for iOs, Android, and Windows, Pocket provides a good way to save the mid– and long-form articles from the web for reading at a more leisurely pace later.
Other options like Feedly: Inoreader (iOS, Android, online) FlowReader (Android, online) NewsBlur (iOS, Android, online)	Other options like Pocket: Diigo (online, iOS, Android) Instapaper (online, iOS, Android) PaperSpan (online, Android) Readability (online, Android, iOS)

How We Read: Engaged and Connected

Troy told me that he was reading Clive Thompson's book *Smarter Than You Think,* and I decided to order it in print so I could share it more easily with my colleagues at work. As I was reading on the train, a particular passage caught my attention, and I knew that I wanted to discuss it with Troy. I quickly pulled out my phone, snapped a picture, and dropped it into a shared photo stream so that Troy could see it [see Figure 3.5]. During our next conversation about the book, we talked about the passage, which Troy found by searching in his digital version of the text. The idea embedded in that shared note guided much of our future conversations about Thompson's book, and it sparked us to invite the author to a Google Hangout, where we further developed our understanding of the text.

As we collaborated on this book over the course of a year, we shared our reading in a variety of ways. We described one example in Chapter 1 using Crocodoc for annotating PDF texts. At other times, while using Flipboard or Feedly to catch up on professional reading, Troy would forward an article to Kristen via email; Kristen, on the other hand, frequently shared links on Facebook and Twitter with Troy. Yet sometimes our reading was in print, and in those cases we used our phones to share in-the-moment thoughts, as Kristen describes. In the case of the Thompson book, Kristen shared only the text, which sparked Troy's own reading. She snapped a picture from the print version of the book (Figure 3.5a), sent it to Troy, and he then pulled up the quote in his Kindle app (Figure 3.5b). You will see this quote—the exact digital text highlighted here, copied straight from the Kindle app—later in this chapter.

In another instance, when Kristen was reading the newly released *Reading Unbound* (Wilhelm & Smith, 2014), which was available only in print format, she annotated a picture using Skitch before texting it to Troy, who did not yet have a copy of the book (Figure 3.6). Using an app that relies on optical character recognition (OCR), Troy was able to pull in the quote from the book that you read in Chapter 2. While this particular method often requires a little editing to clean up typos, it is still a highly effective way to share quotes with others.

Throughout this chapter, we have shared our reading practices, identifying *what* and *where* we read and the underlying choices we make in those areas. Now, as we focus in this section on *how* we read, we consider once again the NCTE policy brief and its roots in a rich history of research into reading instruction. The brief suggests that teachers

Figure 3.5. Figures of print and Kindle versions of Thompson's book.

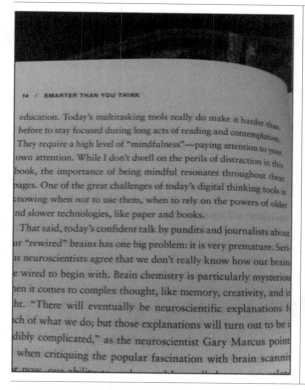

a. Snapshot of Kristen's reading on the train sent to Troy via photo stream.

b. Snapshot of Troy's reading on the Kindle, highlighting and copying the quote.

- Recognize the role of motivation
- Engage in performative response
- Read multiple texts
- Foster engagement
- Encourage choice
- Demonstrate differences in digital and visual texts
- Connect reading and writing
- Develop meaningful discussion

We understand these recommendations to evolve from notions of what adult (expert) readers do, and we know that embedded in this type of instruction will be attention to the strategies employed by expert readers. As research in reading

Figure 3.6. Kristen's snapshot from *Reading Unbound: Why Kids Need to Read What They Want—And Why We Should Let Them* by Jeffrey D. Wilhelm and Michael W. Smith, with Sharon Fransen (2014).

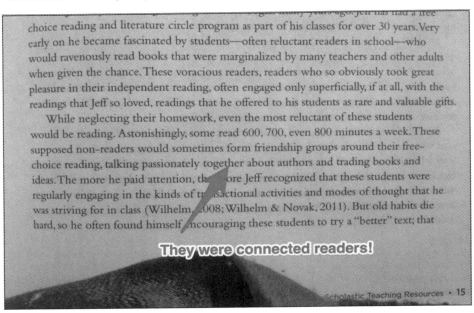

digital texts has revealed—and as both of the profiled readers in this chapter, Sienna and Trevor, demonstrate—these strategies may be different when reading digitally. One key difference we have uncovered as we reflect on our own practices, as well as those of the adolescents in our study, is the increased feasibility of shared reading through digital tools. In short, digital tools connect readers in ways that could not have been imagined before they became available. Therefore, we now outline the specific practices that our surveys of 804 students, 23 interviews, and our own thinking about reading have revealed.

What Are the Practices of Connected Reading?

As we talked with teens about how they read digitally, it became clear that their notion of finding texts is multifaceted, and we now understand from them that "encountering" a text is a separate practice from truly "engaging with" a text. Additionally, we see a practice of "evaluating" that occurs through initial encounters and ongoing engagements with a text. This type of evaluation equates to the idea of "finding value in" and is in addition to notions of judgment about the quality of a text.

Figure 3.7 articulates our view and provides definitions for the practices we learned from these students. Even though they are in chart form, we encourage you to think of these practices not as linear steps in a process but rather as recursive. They are described in more detail in Chapter 4.

Over time we have **encountered** texts in a variety of ways: a newspaper drops on our walkway; we go to the library to find a book; our teacher hands us a copy of a short story; we flip through a magazine to locate the article highlighted on the cover. Today we have many more possibilities as to when and where we may encounter a text. In some cases, we receive the information passively. As both Trevor and Sienna describe, email accounts and social networks bring texts directly to mobile devices and Web browsers with virtually no effort from a reader. In his reflections, Troy describes how various curation tools (such as Feedly) do the work

Figure 3.7. Practices of Connected Reading.

Encountering a Text	
Receiving	Getting a digital text by means of engaging with a website or app (what's in the headlines) or via link from a friend or colleague
Surfing	Skimming and scanning the Internet with little intention, typically for leisure
Stumbling	Following related links or recommendations from social networks, Web services (such as StumbleUpon), or curated websites
Searching	Seeking information actively with specific search terms; comparing and contrasting various websites
Engaging with a Text	
Deciding	Filtering texts to be read or discarded; deciding when and how to read
Curating	Organizing texts for reading and archiving; establishing additional feeds based on current feeds
Reading	Skimming, scanning, digging in; using multimedia; annotating; responding; interacting; monitoring; reading beyond a given text
Sharing	Offering public response to a text; posting or sending it to others
Evaluating a Text	
Determining value	Considering interest, overarching intentions, and immediate purpose to identify how useful the text might be in the moment and in the future; situating the text in a broader, ongoing conversation
Judging	Critiquing the quality of a text (both content and form) as it compares to other similar texts (asking, "Is it a good or bad example of [this particular genre]?")
Employing digital tools	Identifying and utilizing the most appropriate tools to read, annotate, respond to, and share a digital text
Managing distraction	Self-regulating one's attention related to the specific reading task and digital tool in use

of scouring the Web to find relevant texts and deliver them to subscribers. Rather than actively searching for new items to read, we let others (or, perhaps, a search engine's automated tools) do this work for us, and we trust their recommendations. For example, we may skim through our friends' status updates, occasionally clicking on a link. We may get an email newsletter and follow a link to an interesting story. In this way, we consume content shared by others—and others consume content shared by us.

Figure 3.8 shows an example of how sharing leads to encounters within a network of readers. Though Connected Readers often encounter texts that are shared by other readers in their network, they sometimes need to seek content through active search strategies. As Trevor does when he searches purposefully for content related to discussions in Global History, or as Sienna does when she types a particular title into her Kindle library, active searching is an important practice in finding digital texts and in helping readers to move outside of their "filter bubbles" that are limited by friendship circles and the algorithmic programs of the Web (Pariser, 2011). Whether we are researching professional texts for a new article, searching for information on a personally interesting topic, or curious to answer a question raised during dinner conversation, we actively find new texts to read.

Figure 3.8. A sample of "encountering" in one network of readers.

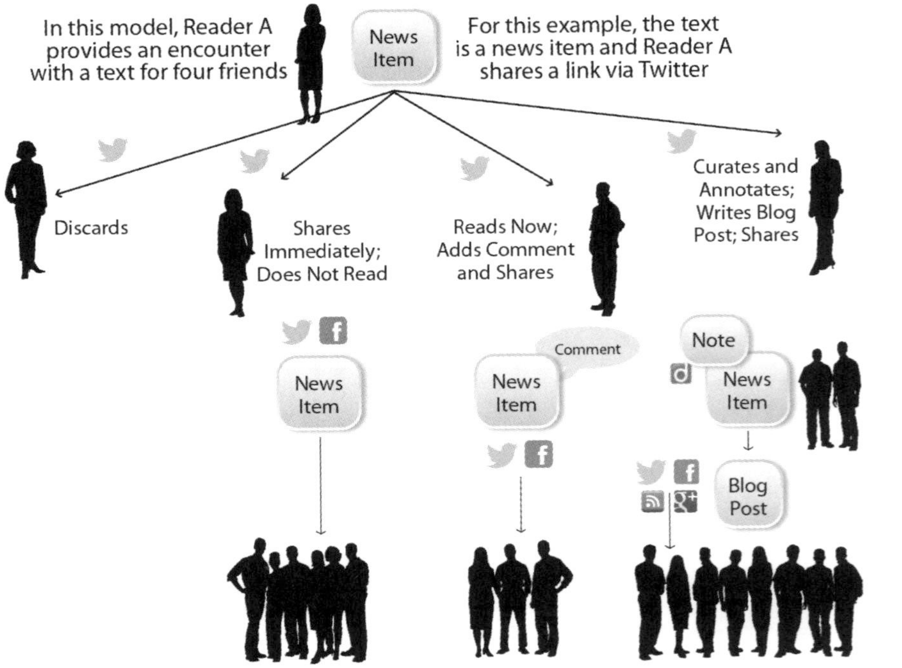

Often these active searches inspire us to set up new feeds, which will in turn deliver us content wherever we choose to read it.

Once we encounter a digital text, we can **engage** with it in a variety of ways. As one of Kristen's reflections indicates, we are often inundated with texts, and probably the first action we take is to determine a path for any given text. This practice involves deciding whether to discard a text completely, to read it immediately, or to save it for later reading (on either the original device or a different device).

Evaluation, or finding value in a text, is a practice that expert readers employ throughout their process of reading. As you (or any reader) determine that a text is one you want to read, you evaluate its value in relation to your purpose for reading. As you decide whether to read it now or later, you consider your immediate interest and context. If you decide to read later, you may curate by saving the text to an app (as Troy describes with his use of Pocket) or by opening a separate tab on your browser (as both Trevor and Kristen do).

If you decide to read immediately, you may employ more traditional reading strategies, such as scanning, skimming, and constructing the gist, and you may also engage in digital opportunities, such as viewing embedded videos, accessing a dictionary feature, and clicking links. As you read, you monitor comprehension and evaluate choices about how they may aid your understanding. You may click links to visit original sources or critique the context in which the work is published. You may decide to create an RSS feed that will deliver new texts to your inbox so that you can read beyond the original text. In short, you evaluate, assigning value to every text you encounter. All of these practices of evaluating a text fuel your reading, and they also contribute to your decision to share the text with other readers in your network.

As the reflections and profiles in this chapter reveal, sharing is key to being a Connected Reader. Whether posting links on Facebook, writing reviews on Goodreads, emailing ideas to others, or even texting a picture of the book to a colleague, public response to reading extends the engagement with a text. And it is through practices of sharing that we often encounter new texts.

Conclusion: Reading Mindfully in a Digital Age

We have articulated practices of Connected Readers, yet we acknowledge the issue brought up by Trevor, who admits that when reading digitally, he is often distracted. In fact, authors such as Bauerlein (2008), who makes claims about teenagers in the "dumbest generation," and Carr (2010), who suggests that society is swimming in an intellectual "shallows" by using the Internet, cite such distraction in making their arguments. However, we understand that digital tools are ubiquitous, and as such, we cannot dismiss them from our lives. Instead, we must develop what Clive

Thompson calls "mindfulness" (2013). Though we shared this passage earlier in the snapshot that Kristen sent Troy as she read Thompson's book on the train (Figure 3.5a), we feel it worth repeating here as evidence of our argument:

> I'm certain that many of these fears are warranted. It has always been difficult for us to maintain mental habits of concentration and deep thought; that's precisely why societies have engineered massive social institutions (everything from universities to book clubs and temples of worship) to encourage us to keep it up. It's part of why only a relatively small subset of people become regular, immersive readers, and part of why an even smaller subset go on to higher education. Today's multitasking tools really do make it harder than before to stay focused during long acts of reading and contemplation. They require a high level of "mindfulness"—paying attention to your own attention. (p. 13, Kindle edition, p. 14 print edition)

This call for "mindfulness" is echoed by a number of other writers engaged in discussions about how to use the Internet effectively, most notably Shirky (2008, 2011), Rheingold (2012), and Davidson (2011), and we believe it is the key to the successful practices of Connected Readers.

In many ways, the practices we outline in this chapter are not new: we have determined paths for individual texts that we encounter; we have curated print books in personal libraries (as Sienna describes); we have read purposefully and mindfully; we have shared our reading in book clubs and with friends and family. What is new, or at least very different, in a digital age is the agency afforded to all readers, especially teen readers, in this process. We encounter many kinds of texts on a daily basis, and we engage with those texts in a variety of ways. Most important, we are connected to other readers at every stage of the game. The context is broader and the opportunities more overwhelming.

As the NCTE policy statement affirms:

> Research shows that reading comprehension depends on a more complex approach. Specifically, reading comprehension results from the integration of two models, text-based and situation-based. The text-based model focuses on the way words are organized into sentences, paragraphs, and whole texts. The situation model refers to the meaning that results from integration of the text-based approach with the reader's prior knowledge and goals. (*RIAS*, p. xii)

We believe we need to adjust our idea of reading so that our students can engage more fully as readers of digital and print texts. For us it is not an either/or (print vs. digital) but a both/and. We realize that the canonical and contemporary books we distribute in school in print form are merely one of the kinds of texts that teens encounter. We imagine that you teach traditional reading strategies that are very useful for these texts, as well as for the texts students find outside of school. At the same time, we must also teach adolescents to think critically and carefully to use digital tools to engage deeply in the texts they will encounter daily.

Moving Teens toward Connected Reading

Nikki, a ninth grader, says that "[Reading] is one of my favorite things to do."

Because "reading's really important for being smart," she does so often, and describes herself as a "pretty driven student" who earns good grades. While she enjoys school, she prefers summer, when she can read completely for herself rather than what she is required to read in school. She enjoys reading large chunks of a book at a time, compared to a little bit before bed each night, and the summer, away from schoolwork, affords her this opportunity.

Though Nikki enjoys reading full-length books in print form, novels make up only a part of her reading life. She reads social networks and news articles digitally. With more than 700 friends on Facebook, she scans status updates and pages, clicking through links that are interesting to her and often reading the articles she finds. When she opens her laptop and fires up her Internet browser, she reads "news stories before doing anything else," even before going on Facebook. She finds a balance between staying informed through the news, engaging in recreational reading, skimming her social networks, and reading required materials for school.

Remember that all links and handouts are located on the companion wiki. Scan this QR code or go to http://connectedreading.wikispaces.com to access Chapter 4 materials.

Nikki reads in both print and digital forms, and she articulates a difference in these contexts. "Because, like you grew up reading print books especially in school, so you're used to reading it so, like, closely, kind of. But when you're online a lot of times you're not reading. You're just like scrolling through stuff." On the other hand, she notes, "I feel like in books, you just read it, and you're done, but with newspapers and magazines, there's a lot more to the story that you didn't hear. . . . So I kind of like using the Internet for that because it's easier to just look up other stuff."

With a dose of reading online, complemented by her deep dives into books, Nikki balances her reading life across the day, across platforms. As she says, "Reading the print book, like even if you do like the book, it's good to be able to have other ways to look at it, kind of like using the Internet to relate to it or, like, understand it better."

Nikki engages in many forms of reading, each kind serving a purpose in her personal and academic lives. We hope you have students who are as adept at Connected Reading as Nikki is, or that reading in this book will help you move readers in this direction. Of course, as we suggested earlier, a number of critics would question Nikki's "scrolling through stuff" and her focus on her social networking, perhaps equating such behaviors with a lack of interest in reading. Our research, however, suggests a different picture of what Nikki and many other teens are doing in their reading lives, online and off.

Rather than painting a monolithic portrait of a generation lost to digital distraction, we see students who are as engaged as ever with reading, although they might not always demonstrate this passion in school. The readers we met as part of our study, readers like Nikki and others we introduce to you in this chapter, deserve to have their own literacy experiences honored and, to our best ability as teachers, enhanced through appropriate instruction. To do so, we have to think critically and creatively about what Connected Reading instruction is and could be for the teens we teach every day.

A Snapshot of Teen Readers Today

To address this issue, we first need to understand what, when, where, why, and how adolescents read. As Smith and Wilhelm (2002) argued,

> If we, as teachers, focused more on the how of reading, our students' experiences in school would more clearly resemble their experience out of school. We would help them develop their competence, which would in turn make them better able to meet the challenge of the texts we ask them to read. (p. 133)

Therefore, we set out to uncover the practices of adolescent readers, specifically their practices related to digital texts. We met Nikki as part of our study, which included visits to twelve classrooms, grades 7–12, in urban, suburban, and rural contexts. As part of this work, we surveyed 804 students and interviewed twenty-three individuals, asking them to discuss their reading, both in and out of school. Smith and Wilhelm conducted similar inquiry more than a decade ago in the research that led to *"Reading Don't Fix No Chevys"* (2002). They used fictional "profiles" of "different kinds of males engaged in embracing or resisting various kinds of literate activity" (p. xxi) to prompt conversations about literacy practices with the adolescent males in their study.

Inspired by their work, we created five fictional profiles of teen readers and asked our participants to respond to the descriptions, highlighting areas where they saw themselves and expanding on those literacy practices. You can read our profiles in Appendix C and may find them useful for sharing with your own students. We found that once students started talking about Sally, Maggie, Robin, Tabitha, and Alexandra (or their male counterparts), they easily reflected on their own reading habits.

The analysis of the survey and interview data led us to the creation of our model of Connected Reading that we illustrate in Chapter 2, and in an effort to capture a picture of this population of teen readers, we share here what we uncovered in relation to *what*, *why*, and *how* teens read digitally. We begin by thinking about reading *contexts*, then we consider the nature of the *texts* themselves, and finally we explore the effect of student *interest* as influences on reading behaviors. Then we highlight the practices of Connected Readers. (A revised version of our survey, appropriate for classroom instruction, is referenced in Chapter 6 and also included in Appendix B. It is also available on our wiki as a Google Form template.) Throughout this chapter, we introduce you to more of the readers we met during the course of this study.

Flexibility in Context

> I usually click on [a link] and read the title, see how relevant it is, kind of skim it, and if it's good I read it. And then I usually print it out, not because I need to read it [that way] but because we usually have to hand in a hard copy to the teacher. (Kelly, grade 9)

Kelly presents an interesting dichotomy in her reading life: when assigned by her teacher to find an article, she searches for and then reads the online text, but she is required to bring a print version of that text to the classroom. Given the options for finding, in this case, "a current event article," it is important to note the decisions that Kelly makes. She considers contextual factors that include whether to locate the article in print or via a digital source, and she determines her interest in the topic before reading.

Based on research into the digital habits of teens, it does not surprise us that Kelly decides to find the text digitally, despite the fact that she knows she needs a

checks Twitter, Pinterest, and Tumblr and sometimes uses her phone to do so. She mostly uses her phone for "purposes for school and reading and actually, like trying to get ahold of people, so, like texting them if I need help." She has a Kindle app on her phone, and she has downloaded all of her books from her Kindle Fire to it. She also has Lumosity, which she uses for school, and her teacher's wiki, as well as her Gmail, Google Drive, and Goodreads apps. She likes "to put little posts and comments to the books that people read" on Goodreads. Kristy also reads fan fiction, and she has written her own fan fiction. For Kristy, reading is "when you read more than five pages . . . or like more than ten." Though she admits that she must read them to respond, in her view emails, text messages, and social network posts are not "real reading."

Kristy is a reader, and like many of the teens in our study, she reads a variety of digital texts. From our sample, 84 percent said that they read content from the Internet such as news stories and blogs.[1] When asked if they read digital books or magazines, 50 percent responded yes.[2] Finally, 82 percent said they had at least one social network account (e.g., Facebook, Twitter, Google), and though we did not specifically ask this on the survey, every student we interviewed who owns a mobile phone engages in texting. We can safely assume that nearly all of these teens read these brief messages, composed as "writing-by-the-way" (Hicks & Perrin, 2014), in a similar manner: quickly composed and even more quickly read.

Though 54 percent of survey respondents acknowledge that the reading they do in text messaging and on social networks is in fact reading, many others agree with Kristy, noting that this kind of reading is something different from "real reading." As Emily says, "To be honest, I don't really consider the short-forms as reading because I consider reading more of, like sitting down and reading a book or a magazine and, like actually learning from it." The idea that "real reading" is connected to making meaning (or learning) surfaces several times in the data, and it seems for many adolescents, as Nikki argues, "If you're reading like a status or whatever, you're not looking for the meaning, and most times there isn't any meaning."

This negative view of texting and social networking is common in popular media (Thurlow, 2006), and given the results of the Pew study, in which teens reported that they did not view this type of writing as "real writing" (Lenhart et al., 2008), we are not surprised that nearly half the sample do not view their practices in these media as reading.

In an attempt to recast this view of what we read, we turn again to Clive Thompson. In a 2010 piece in *Wired Magazine*, Thompson discusses a prevalence of tweets and text messages:

> We're often told that the Internet has destroyed people's patience for long, well-thought-out arguments. . . . [However,] I think something much more complex and

interesting is happening: The torrent of short-form thinking is actually a catalyst for more long-form meditation. (para. 1)

Thompson connects thinking and writing by outlining three forms of text: short-form, middle-form, and long-form. He describes short-form writing as "often half-baked or gossipy and may not even be entirely true" (para. 3), and he contrasts it to long-form writing, which might be "a deeply considered report and analysis, and it often takes weeks, months, or years to produce" (para. 4). Thompson argues that short-forms are simply first drafts that may lead to deeper conversations about a topic. In other words, status updates, tweets, and text messages are conversational, and as such they represent first-draft thinking; however, with the opportunity for written response and feedback, these first drafts can be developed into longer pieces. Finally, Thompson suggests that middle-form thinking, which is "neither fast enough to be conversational nor slow enough to be truly deep," is being displaced by the flurry of short-form activity (para. 6). He cites *Time* and *Newsweek* articles as examples of middle-form writing, the kinds of reports that summarize facts and offer some analysis as well.

Thompson's claims about these three types of digital text and the thinking they invoke made us question our own reading practices. Both of us read dozens, perhaps hundreds of short-form pieces of writing each day: text messages and instant messages from family, friends, and colleagues; status updates and Twitter feeds from our social and professional networks; headlines and titles from RSS feeds and browser searches. We also read long-form writing in digital form: professional articles, extended essays on blogs, and books or ebooks. We see these kinds of reading in Kristy's profile as well.

We admit, however, that the majority of our own reading is somewhere in between fast, conversational flow and deep contemplation. We engage as readers with most blog posts and news articles differently than we do with the other kinds of texts mentioned in the previous paragraph, and often we are led to these texts by our short-form reading. For all of these forms of digital reading, we, as adult readers, are connected to other readers in ways that teens might not be—and they may not even realize the potential of digital tools to do so. So even though Kristy reads short-forms, she doesn't see them as reading, and she may not engage with them in thoughtful ways that lead her to deeper encounters with texts or connections with other readers.

In Figure 4.2, we extend Thompson's idea of short-, mid-, and long-form types of writing in order to categorize various types of digital texts. Each of these three forms presents new and interesting challenges for readers who must constantly make choices about what to read and how to navigate the seemingly infinite number of texts at their fingertips.

Figure 4.2. Examples of short-, middle -, and long-form digital texts.

Short-Form	Mid-Form	Long-Form
Public social network posts • Character limited (such as Twitter) • Character unlimited (such as Facebook) • Captions on images (such as Instagram) • Comments on other status updates Short snippets or summaries • Search engine results • Summaries on news aggregators such as Yahoo News or MSN • "Headlines" in an RSS reader or magazine-style reader such as Flipboard or Zite Messages and digitalk • Direct messages and texts • Chat rooms and other forums	Online journalism • Brief stories from reputable sources, typically 100–1,000 words, but up to 5,000 words, and may include audio or video supplements (see http://medium.com) Blog posts • Posts from personal or group blogs, also approximately 100–1,000 words Specific Web-based articles • Articles posted to an edited and curated website from an organizational, corporate, or educational institution Fiction • Fiction, fan fiction, or hypertext fiction pieces	"Longform" journalism • Longer stories from reputable sources, typically 5,000 words or more, and may include audio or video supplements (see http://longform.org) Academic articles • Articles that have been peer reviewed and published to a journal. These articles may be in an open access journal or available only through database subscription. Ebooks and transmedia • Longer pieces of fiction and nonfiction that are presented as a cohesive whole, yet will likely require more than one sitting to read fully
These kinds of texts are often skimmed or scanned. Readers glance at them, consuming in a way that does not involve deep cognitive engagement. Often these texts are intended to be conversational.	These texts require more cognitive engagement and usually take longer to read, anywhere from 5–20 minutes. These texts can typically be read and comprehended in one sitting.	These texts require deep cognitive engagement or extended reading time, usually more than one sitting. Whether the texts are literature or nonfiction, readers must employ multiple strategies over time to comprehend them.

As teachers we find ourselves in a world where reading is ubiquitous, and we must consider the work that our students are doing outside of school so we can help them to establish mindful, savvy reading practices. Moving from short- to middle- to long-form writing is an important practice of Connected Readers, one we hope teens will do mindfully rather than spontaneously.

Interest Matters

Leo describes himself as "just an average high school student" who tends to procrastinate. He reads articles online that he finds from his social network feeds or the MSN homepage, which he sees every time he logs out of his email. A picture or an interesting headline will often capture his attention and entice him to read further. Full-length books, however, he rarely reads, and he readily admits that though he has started them all, he has not finished many of the texts he is assigned for school because they lose his interest. For the last independent reading assignment of his senior year, Leo chose a particular book to earn an extra credit point; but he "wasn't too interested in it," and he didn't actually read the text to complete the assignment. Instead, he read summaries online and literary articles about the book. When he reads, he prefers digital texts, which he finds help keep him focused and organized.

Outside of school, teens read what interests them, and, as Leo's profile highlights, they often abandon academic texts that do not fit this category. Often they read short-forms from their friends because they are interested in connecting socially. They seek out mid- and long-forms based on other interests. As one survey respondent said, "I like to read from news applications like Flipboard because I can see news related to things that I am interested in."

As we outlined in Chapter 3, short-form reading often leads the two of us, as adult readers, to mid-forms, and we generally begin our professional and personal digital reading by skimming feeds. The teens in our sample use similar strategies. They skim status updates; news and Twitter feeds; Instagram, Facebook, and Google+ posts; captions; comments; headlines; and text messages looking for individuals, words, or images that interest them. As Heather says of her practice of reading on Twitter, "If I see a word that catches my eye, then I'll read their tweet."

Heather goes on to explain how connections in these social spaces contribute to her motivation to read beyond short-form. She describes her reading related to devastating tornados in the Midwest:

Somebody knew somebody else who was in Oklahoma and they—their house was taken away, sadly. But they posted that they survived and they were part of helping the cleanup and stuff like that. So that's where I read the article. Like they posted the article about their friend, and I clicked on it and got to read, . . . [So if it's] somebody trying to get their feelings out, and I care about that person, like I'll read the whole thing and try to relate to them and help them out, but if it's really long, like somebody was writing their own little novel online, I probably wouldn't end up reading the whole thing, because if it didn't catch my interest and things like that I wouldn't finish it off.

Though we have heard suggestions from teachers that teens are abandoning social media sites like Facebook as adult users enter the virtual space, the data from our survey indicate that students in grades 7–12 are still using the popular site. As Catrina admits, "It's addicting," or perhaps, as Robert says, "It is a hassle to stay in the whole social media, but I am still a part of it just because I don't want to be out of the loop." Short-form reading connects teens with one another; it's conversational; it's social. Understanding that this type of reading is done for different purposes— and that it can lead to more engaged, thoughtful reading—is a challenge for all of us as readers in a digital age, and even more so for us as teachers of reading.

Like the work of Wilhelm and Smith (2014), our data confirm that kids read what interests them. In fact, 45 percent of our survey respondents said they like to read a great deal, and another 32 percent like it some. Nearly eight of ten teenagers enjoy reading! Forty-nine percent of our sample say they read for themselves (albeit mostly outside of school) every day.

These statistics are not quite as impressive when the students think about the reading they do for school. Though half of the sample's students say they enjoy reading at least "some," only 10 percent enjoy the reading they do for school a great deal. As Leo indicates, if teens are not interested, they are not likely to actually do the reading that is assigned. This claim is not a new one; we have known for years that interest matters. Now we must consider how to engage teen readers in the vast amounts of interesting texts available to them in digital contexts.

Practices of Connected Reading

> I'll generally read a little bit in each paragraph to see if it's something that interests me, and if it is, I'll read the whole thing. If it's not, I'll just kind of like get the gist of it. If it's a little bit boring in some sections, I'll move on. (Andrew, grade 12)

At the time of his interview, Andrew was a senior who was very clear that he prefers print books to digital reading. He finds reading off a Kindle or an iPad to be "physically restricting," and overall, not cost effective. An avid reader who has read many of Robin Hobb's books, such as the Farseer trilogy, Andrew also acknowledges an "innate problem" with his reading life. He likes having the "resources available" to him on the Internet, even though he would rather read in print, and he frequently searches for information on topics he is interested in online, never going to the library to find books.

Andrew participates in deviantART (www.deviantart.com), an online community where individuals can post their own artwork, write journals related to their art, and give and receive feedback. It is his reading in this community that is captured in the quote at the beginning of this section; Andrew has a clear strategy for interacting with the journals he chooses to read. He is also mindful about his practices for looking for art:

> You have the main page and there's a little thumbnail of every picture that's been recently posted. There's like sixty on a page. And you skim through and you're like, "Hey, I like this picture. I want to see it." You don't want to click on the picture, be redirected, look at the picture, like it or don't like it, then go back to the previous page. Hold down control, click on all the icons you like, and then go through all the pages that you have open. Like this, like this, like this, don't like this.

Andrew has combined traditional reading strategies (skimming, scanning, and constructing the gist) with his understanding of the technological tools that will help him to read and respond. He uses scrolling, keyboard functions, and multiple tabs to help him navigate the texts and to make his response more efficient. We believe that Andrew has developed some Connected Reading practices: he curates his social network; he locates information through active searches; he reads with intentionality and uses digital tools effectively to support his comprehension; and he responds to what he reads, connecting to others.

We found that many of the teens in our sample, like Andrew, have strategies for engaging with digital texts. We also found that many feel overwhelmed and distracted by the possibilities of the Internet and therefore do not engage in mindful practices.

Encountering a Digital Text

> I do not choose what I read. Most of the time, something will show up on a website, and it will be interesting, and I go on and read the article. (survey respondent)

Given the abundance of information that students face each time they log in to the Internet, it is important that teens develop mindful practices for selecting texts. We know that teens choose to read what interests them, but how are they encountering texts? Are they, like the survey respondent quoted here, simply clicking on links that appear in front of them, or do some of them have more mindful practices?

We learned from our participants that they find texts in four ways: receiving, stumbling, purposeful searching, and surfing (see Chapter 3 for definitions). Most of the time, they receive them without doing more than opening their app or browser. As Trevor says, "When you sign into Yahoo, [the article] is already there." In fact, both Leo and Dee admit they would never purposefully search for news articles, but since "the news is right there" (Dee) when they open Yahoo or sign out of a Web-based email, they "follow the top stories" (Leo).

We think of this type of encounter as passive since it requires little effort on the reader's part. Every student we interviewed and many that we surveyed indicate that the majority of texts they encounter come from social network feeds and simply appear when they log in to their accounts. As they move from these passive encounters into more active practices, we found slight differences in the ways the teens find various reading material. We have categorized these into stumbling, purposeful searching, and surfing.

Heather practices all three to find digital texts. She often begins by checking email through AOL, and then she moves to the recommended stories that appear in her browser. Sometimes she continues on to surf the World Wide Web, moving from site to site with no clear purpose, especially if she is bored. Finally, she describes how she often searches for particular information when she is eating dinner with friends and family:

Heather: If I was ever in a discussion and trying to prove my own point, . . . I end up probably looking up what I'm trying to prove, or like if I'm talking about something and trying to explain it, but I can't really, I'll try to look it up on my phone and try to find a picture of whatever I'm talking about.

Kristen: And where would you go to look it up?

Heather: I'd go onto my Safari app and probably just type it into the search bar at the top and look it up like that. And if I can't find it immediately on the first page, then I just pretty much give up.

Kristen: And you would click on one of those links based on what?

Heather: Based on if it was like a handy, a reliable site.

Most of the teens we interviewed indicated that they receive information through social networks or by active searches and "careful use of Google keywords," and several suggested that they often evaluate the credibility of the sites they find. Alan has clearly defined practices that include stumbling, searching, and surfing:

> If I'm just bored or if I need like a recipe to cook something, I'll go on the Internet, like "Let's try chuck steak, let's try that." Or if I'm just bored, I need something to do. Or a current event assignment for economics or government, I'll go to the *Wall Street Journal, New York Times*, or CNN, and I'll just go and look up something. Or I'll just look up a video that I remember from when I was younger, and I'll click it into YouTube and I'll just watch a video.

Alan indicates that he surfs the Web when he is "bored," but he also does purposeful searching using specific news sites, Google, or YouTube. For his academic work, specifically in looking for current events articles, he follows a specific process of purposeful searching. He begins on CNN, and then, he says, "If I don't find anything, I'll go on Google." He decides to read an article based on "how much information there is. If it's specific. If it gives important detail and it gives accurate feedback of scientists and people who have read the article before and their opinions on it."

In analyzing the data, we noticed a difference in intentionality between stumbling and surfing (though we do recognize that there is some overlap in these categories and one may lead to the other in any given sitting). Based on how the students describe their reading, we see stumbling as a slightly more intentional form of surfing. Surfing involves browsing from link to link, from website to website, consuming various kinds of content along the way. Stumbling, on the other hand, includes the same practices but within curated boundaries and usually with an intentional purpose. For example, one survey respondent said,

> I like to choose my digital reading from the sources that interest me. I use sources such as Pulse newspaper on my iPod to find interesting articles related to men's health and upcoming technology. I also scatter through CNN, Yahoo, and other news sources for articles from the media.

This teen demonstrates what we call stumbling, following links he receives via a feed in an app called Pulse (since purchased by LinkedIn and renamed LinkedIn Pulse) that he has curated to focus on two topics of interest. He also stumbles ("scatters") through particular curated websites with this same intentionality. We understand this intentionality to be about mindfulness in reading.

For the most part, the adolescents in our study reported reading short-forms they receive passively, usually in the form of status updates from friends on social networks. Few seemed to have developed practices of curation that enable stumbling, though many did describe practices of stumbling within their social networks and various news sites. We think it important that though they articulated intentions that included connecting with peers, the teens themselves felt little purpose when reading short-forms, or as Catrina said, "It's just like this stupid mindless stuff that you just read. I don't know how to describe it. Like, there's nothing, like, that's so important that I need to read it. It's just, it just happens." They consume a lot, but they may not be doing so mindfully—and they may not realize that digital tools can help them to curate in a way that keeps them focused on a given purpose, reducing the risk of distraction.

Engaging with a Digital Text

Once readers encounter a digital text, they may choose to engage with it. The teens in our study helped us to identify practices that include deciding, curating, reading, and sharing. We want to stress that these processes are not linear in nature; however, we break them down here for purposes of illustration.

Deciding and Curating

> **Dee:** Pinterest is my main thing. I usually focus on four sections—like I'll go fashion, hair, and I wind up—I'll pin whatever I like. . . .
>
> **Kristen:** So do you click through and look at the actual article or you just repin the picture that you like?
>
> **Dee:** Repin the picture. The only thing that I—what I do is I'll do a bunch and then if I remember later on, then I'm going to go look at my board, which you create. And then I go through that, and if I'm picking prom hair stuff, and like my appointment's

in a week or something, I'm going to go back to that board and just look at those.

. . .

Kristen: Are you reading, because I know that sometimes there's captions or people will post a comment. Do you read those things?

Dee: Oh yeah. If it says like—if sometimes they'll say like "Read now, pin later." Sometimes I'll click and then it brings you into. . . . Like the fitness stuff is cool. If I see something with fitness and . . . it'll bring you to *Fitness* magazine, like for certain exercises, I'll go to that. And then I'll look at the exercises, but if it's an exercise I don't like, then I'm just going to exit out of it and go back to what I was doing.

Dee finds digital texts by stumbling through Pinterest, but her description of her process captures additional engagement with some of those texts. She pins them for later reference. This act of curation allows her to save particular reading for later, and it is part of her decision-making process for determining the path she will take with a given text. Dee also notes that she will easily discard an article if it doesn't interest her.

The teens in our sample evaluate texts and decided whether to read immediately, save for later, or discard completely based on two factors: (1) if the text interests them and (2) if they are required to read it for school. Often interest trumps all, and as Leo revealed earlier in this chapter, if a student isn't interested in the assigned reading, he or she is unlikely to complete it.

Most students talk about Facebook and other social networks as the basis for their online reading. They scan through status updates and focus on individuals, either because they have an emotional connection or because they often find their posts interesting. One survey respondent shares very specific time-management strategies:

> I choose to read my texts [Short Message Service messages, or SMS] first because it's my personal life closest to me, and I spend about a minute every five reading them. Next would be my random Google questions in the day about curiosity questions I have come up, and I spend about five minutes three times a day on that. The last would be CNN because I'm so curious as to what's happening out there in the world. I spend about a good half an hour on that.

This student moves from receiving to purposeful searching to stumbling with very specific purposes, but she also suggests intentionality in what she chooses to read in the moment. Another participant describes his choices in deciding to read any given digital text:

I tend to read from forums such as Reddit because they usually have to offer that which I am interested in. When it comes to non-forum posts, I tend to ignore that which I find of little importance or minor interest to me, although I will glance at something that is able to grab my interest. On occasion, I will go searching for something interesting, and will read everything link-by-link so as to absorb as much information as possible. I will also further research that which takes a strong hold of my interest, even if it is not of significant importance.

Most of the students indicate they either read a text immediately or skip it altogether. We found very few of them curating texts for later. We think this lack of intentionality in curating may be linked to the fact that they do most of their reading in the moment and that they don't realize curation can lead them to more interesting texts in the future. As one respondent said, finding and deciding to read texts is "mainly an accidental process." Without intentionality in decision making, not only is distraction possible, but it is also likely that a reader will miss important digital texts.

Reading

Teens report that they draw on many traditional reading strategies to tackle difficult digital texts. They scan, summarize, and take notes. They use context clues to figure out words they don't know and ask a teacher or adult to help when stuck. They also reread text they do not understand. They use the strategies we as teachers of literacy know and love, and interestingly, they use them mindfully for short-, middle-, and long-form reading. One survey respondent explains,

> If I cannot understand a text [SMS message], I either keep rereading it or ask someone, "What does it mean?" so I can understand. For example, if someone is texting you something disrespectful and you reread it to make sure, . . . you keep rereading it and making sure you don't see what you was just seeing. And if you are reading a book, there comes a sentence or word you don't understand, so you ask someone like a teacher near you to help you because you don't want to go on; you want to understand what you are reading in the book.

This student demonstrates the fluidity of reading across digital and print texts and the ability to draw on print-based strategies when reading digitally. One reading strategy that seems particularly important to the teen readers is reading beyond the text. Many of the participants explain that they follow links or actively search additional resources to support their reading of a given text. For example, they suggest that they look for summaries online, going to "YouTube, CliffsNotes, and other websites that contain factual information," creating for themselves, as the following survey respondent indicates, a browser-full of "teachers":

I search it up online or ask a teacher if they can explain what the author is trying to say. I look for videos on YouTube and see if anyone talked about the book. Sometimes Tumblr is a great teacher because Tumblr is basically a blog but with pictures. All I would do is search the book, and I would get all kinds of different interpretations from different people. Eighty percent of the time I use Tumblr to help me out with everything.

In many ways, the ease with which they can employ this strategy of reading beyond the text empowers students. As one participant suggests,

I'm open to more information than I'm usually given in school because most teachers present texts to kids saying that they have to form their own static opinions, don't think outside the box, and follow strict rules on how to reply. Being online makes me feel like I have some form of control of my life, and makes me read more and better.

This student identifies a sense of agency in out-of-school reading that is created, in part, by the ability to move beyond a text.

Though we could identify various strategies that teens use when reading digital texts, what we did not see in the data were clear strategies for annotating digital texts, nor did we find evidence that students are connected during reading in meaningful ways that allow others to help them make meaning. In some cases, it seems as though students do not know that tools exist to help them in these ways. For example, one student says,

Digital reading I think is better suited to less challenging texts as it is more difficult or impossible to annotate. If it is the type of text for which I would be reading for an assignment or for comprehension, I take notes, but usually paper notes, especially if the type of digital reading is on the computer, because flipping windows on a computer is annoying and messes with concentration.

This response touches on students' lack of familiarity with digital tools that are part of Connected Reading in a digital age, but it also suggests an important element of digital reading: distraction. Though it has always been possible for a reader to become distracted while engaged in a text, digital opportunities make mindfulness even more important. Perhaps the words of this participant best sum up the possibilities of distraction:

Those freaking links! They are so distracting. If I am online reading articles, my whole train of thought can be disrupted because a link in the text seems interesting, and I don't want to forget to click on it or lose where it was. Usually when I do that, and I click on a link, I try to make sure I open it in a new tab so that I can read it later; otherwise I'll never even get back to the original article. Even if I do remember to open the interesting links in a new tab, there are enough so that it's still a distracting mess.

One way that we as adults limit distractions in our professional reading is to open multiple tabs and save interesting links for later reading, much like we might stack a pile of books from the library and read them one at a time. A few students also mentioned this practice, and the teens also said they use digital tools to substitute for other traditional reading strategies. For example, some teens use a mouse cursor to track their place in the text as they read (similar to finger tracking); others use highlighting tools; many look up words they don't know using Google, or Dictionary.com, or, as one student says, "Siri, if I am on my iPad/iPod." These tools help them to navigate and comprehend a text. As one student suggests,

> With these unique opportunities in reading online, there is much more room for complete comprehension. If you read an article that uses words you don't know, you can look them up and understand what they are saying. If there is a detailed process that is difficult to convey through text, pictures and videos are at your fingertips. Even if there aren't videos and pictures, there is still a great deal of other sources that are available to find a better explanation.

We agree with this teen's assessment, and we were surprised that so few tools surfaced in the survey responses and interviews. We know adult readers who regularly employ keyboard shortcuts, manipulate font size, use apps to remove clutter and ads, and engage a variety of other tools that support comprehension and minimize distraction. (We share some of these tools in the next few chapters.) We are not convinced, however, that teens are aware of these possibilities.

Sharing

> I have the [Tumblr] app on my phone. I will go through it and read it, and if I like any pictures, I'll reblog it. (Heather, grade 12)

As we argued earlier, reading has always been social. As readers of print books, we share our reading with others just as Kristen and her family members have physically shared hard copies of novels for years. The teens in our sample are no different. As one individual says, to share her reading, "I just talk to people who I know are reading or have read the book," and several of the survey respondents said they share via word of mouth and class discussions.

This sharing takes on a new dimension in Connected Reading because of the vast network of opportunities for both reading and responding. Not all students share their reading, choosing instead to keep their engagement private, but those who do share use a variety of digital tools, including social networks, blogs, instant and text messaging services, and email. They use Google Docs, screenshots, and a variety of websites, such as Goodreads, BookTube (YouTube), Reddit, and Quotev. Others with particular interests have found interest-based networks for sharing, such as Asianfanfics, and Writing.Com. Like Kristen and her family, they share copies of books—but on Nooks and Kindles that are shared. One student sums up the importance of her social connection in her reading: "I absolutely LOVE to share the books I just read. Especially if they're good. I write it on my Goodreads account; I share it to my friends on Facebook; or if someone is in the same Fandom as I, I recommend it to them. I really love talking about books."

We found the variety of tools used to share reading interesting, but we also found it curious that only 8 percent of the students have an account devoted to discussing their reading experiences, and 68 percent of the sample has never heard of Goodreads, Shelfari, or any other network where they can share their long-form reading. Even those who report having a social network account told us that they did not discuss their reading using that network. While we can only speculate, we wonder if it is "uncool" to discuss reading on Facebook or Twitter, at least from a teenager's perspective.

We also ponder why only one teen in the entire study notes the social connection she can make during reading: "The Kindle takes the book a step further. They show what lines in the book people have highlighted to show the more important quotes." This element of Connected Reading is a key advantage of digital tools and one we highlight in later chapters related to instructional strategies.

Evaluating throughout Reading

As educators, any time we hear the term *evaluate* we typically think about grades, rubrics, report cards, and, more recently, systems used to rate teachers. We recognize that evaluation is part of the fabric of education, and we want to be clear about how we are discussing "evaluating texts" in our model of Connected Reading. First, an example; then a definition.

> It's kind of hypocritical in a way because I do like digital reading because it's so easy, but then I also think that after a while, there's going to be less and less books published because people know that it's going to be—that digital reading will probably be better. But then the other thing is . . . I've tried searching for books on the digital reading, but some aren't available. They're usually just available in paperback form. And like I said before, for text messaging and things like that, it's kind of like a different language. So I feel like it's getting less and less formal in a way. (Emily, grade 9)

In this description, Emily is working through her beliefs about what it means to read and how reading changes in different spaces. She is struggling to make sense of her "hypocritical" feelings about digital reading compared to paperbacks while also trying to balance the idea that texts are "like a different language," one that is "getting less and less formal." These moments of tensions are, we argue, more than just about how to encounter and engage with print or digital texts; instead, they are moments when Emily is placing a value on her own reading practices and the types of texts she needs or wants to read.

In this sense, then, "evaluating" a print or digital text becomes more than simply determining the credibility of an author, the accuracy of information, or how exciting the plot of a particular story happens to be (though all of these practices are also part of evaluating). Instead, evaluating in a model of Connected Reading becomes a chance for adolescent readers to make judgment calls about themselves as readers and what they choose to do in their reading practices. In this way, evaluation is an act of agency. Our teen readers are trying to balance the demands of being successful readers with the expectations that their peers, parents, teachers, and other stakeholders have of them.

Therefore, we define *evaluating*—as it relates to reading practices, both print and digital—as a process, sometimes instantaneous and sometimes lengthy, of placing value on a text. More than just asking, "Is this a good book, website, or text message?," the readers we interviewed instead would ask, "What will this book, website, or text message do for me? What do I bring to this digital text?" Connected Readers, we argue, do this kind of evaluation from the moment of encounter and throughout their reading.

In the examples we share throughout this chapter, we see evaluation taking place as teens make decisions about the value of a text on the first encounter. They make an initial judgment about whether to read a text, especially digital texts, and then make ongoing judgments throughout reading. These judgments include continuing with or abandoning a text, comparing and contrasting a text to others, and gauging the credibility of the author and accuracy of the information.

We also see evaluation through context, which includes elements of when, what, and how to read. As many of the readers discussed in this book demonstrate, readers make choices between print and digital texts, between schoolwork and pleasure reading, between looking up an unfamiliar word or just forging ahead. Context can make a significant difference in how a student chooses to engage with a text. For instance, Sienna explains how her reading contexts differ:

> I use the public library, and I used the dictionary feature a lot, which I found has been a really—and so I find the Kindles are really a good way to read more challenging subject matter. Rather, because you can look up words easier and like right now I'm reading *Brave New World* like in print in the actual book form. And I found that there's a lot of words that I don't understand because they might be more medical terms, and so I've been writing them down, but it's easier when you can get the instant gratification of looking it up.

Sienna demonstrates evaluation through context, which in this case includes the tool–text connection (dictionary) that will enable her to engage with more challenging texts.

Finally, we see evaluation through purpose and intention, categories that focus on the *why* of reading. With purpose, we consider the reader's ultimate goal for any reading session that can, of course, shift and change in process. For instance, one of Alan's goals included spending thirty minutes to search the Web for information on a particular topic in order to find resources for a research project on climate change, specifically related to current scientific predictions. In contrast, intention would be broader in scope. A reader's intention would be about larger aims and hopes, an idea guiding the specific purpose. For example, as Alan searches for specific information on climate change, he is also pleased to find other information about weather and climate patterns. If purpose is a short-term goal for one reading event, then intention guides a reader's trajectory over time. Evaluating through purpose and intention helps readers to manage distractions and to engage deeply with texts.

We believe that evaluating is one of the most important practices of Connected Reading and that it is through evaluation that readers achieve the goals of the principles of Connected Learning—interest powered, academically oriented, peer supported, openly networked, and with shared purpose (Ito et al., 2013).

"Reading is supposed to be . . . connective"

> So I like doing the mid-form articles because it's like enough to read where you're interested, but not so much where you're overwhelmed. . . . It seems like it's just kind of easier to do the short-form because there's a lot more of that on Facebook and stuff. And it's not very time-consuming. Like if I want to read a mid-form something, I have to kind of set it, like make sure I don't have to jump up and do something else. I have to sit there for like ten minutes where I can read it. But for like Facebook or something, you can just scroll through and stop as you want. But for the mid-form reading, you have to sit there more and just read through it. (Nikki, grade 9)

We return to Nikki because she captures a difference between short- and mid-form texts. Mid-form reading requires more cognitive engagement than does short-form, yet we wonder how (and if) students are actually making that shift.

Analyzing the interviews and survey data helped us to define the practices of Connected Readers, and we were impressed with the variety of strategies that teens have developed to sift through the information they encounter, to manage distractions while reading, and to share their reading with others. Many of these adolescents have begun to develop into Connected Readers, yet we found that most strategies used by teens simply transferred print practices or, at best, augmented them through use of digital tools. Very few participants indicated a shift in their practices that accounts for the seamlessness of digital texts and tools.

For instance, many of the students we have highlighted so far have mentioned the strategy of using the dictionary to look up a word. How many of them considered sharing the sentence they were reading as a status update or tweet, asking their peers for feedback on what this word or phrase could mean in this context, or discussing the implications of this word choice in the given text? While noting that they are connected to a network of peers, few students indicated that they would rely on their peers for help in the meaning-making process.

This seamlessness, in both using the tools and connecting to the network, is particularly important during the act of reading. Digital tools allow readers to connect inside a text while they are reading. These kinds of shared readings contribute to meaning making, and they might support struggling readers as they engage with complex or challenging texts. Perhaps even more important, however, is intentionality. We are not convinced that the majority of teens have developed mindful practices of evaluation that take into account their contexts, the tools and texts available to them, and their varied purposes and intentions for reading. If we are to adopt a model of Connected Reading, we must recognize the particular comprehension skills that are crucial at different stages of a reader's development. We do not want to simply co-opt Connected Learning (Ito et al., 2013) to make it more "schooly," yet we also do not want to ignore the academic nature of our task as teachers.

This distinction was important as we considered the role of digital reading in our own lives and in society in general. We know that more and more reading is being done on a screen. As more and more schools are moving to one-to-one adoption of tablets and digital textbooks, we are afraid that this move is happening without full consideration of what it means to read digitally. If we want our students to become Connected Readers, we must meet them where they are and help them to navigate the variety of devices and texts they will encounter both academically and socially.

The adolescents highlighted in this chapter are diverse readers—some highly digital, some not; some highly connected, some not; and some highly engaged, while others just don't see themselves as readers. It is our job as teachers to reach all of these students and to prepare them to navigate mindfully the various kinds of texts they will encounter. In the next two chapters, we discuss practices that we— and the colleagues we have been fortunate enough to visit in classrooms this past year—have found effective in keeping students attentive and engaged in reading. We understand that not all texts are digital, yet, as Andrew says, "Reading is supposed to be . . . connective." We hope that all classrooms will use digital tools in an effort to create Connected Readers.

**Chapter
Five**

Using Digital Tools
with Print Texts

According to my NYC high school students, it's not cool to read a book while riding the subway. After years of trying to sell their long commutes as a great time to read, I stopped issuing them books. Instead, I gave students the option of taking a hard copy or receiving digital copies of the book. On nights when we have assigned reading, I send the excerpts to students' school email. They may think it's uncool to read a book on the train, but it looks really cool to be doing something on your phone for an hour . . . even if it is a few pages of *Lord of the Flies*! (Lauren, English teacher)

The walls of Lauren's classroom are filled with colorful easel sheets, like the one in Figure 5.1, that have been created with her students and using her students' work. The room itself is like many other classrooms across the city: a chalkboard lines the front; desks form a double U around the perimeter; a library of books sits clearly organized against the windows. The only digital technology evident is on the cart at the front of the room that holds Lauren's

Figure 5.1. Mastery of close reading poster from Lauren's classroom.

Remember that all links and handouts are located on the companion wiki. Scan this QR code or go to http://connectedreading.wikispaces.com to access Chapter 5 materials.

laptop and a projector. There is no Smartboard; there are no tablets or computers; students are not permitted to bring devices into the school. However, Lauren uses her projector daily, and she has created space for her students to read and write online, knowing they have access via their phones and devices outside of school. As she describes in the chapter-opening vignette, she blends print and digital texts both to engage her students and because she believes it is important that they learn to communicate professionally by using digital tools.

When Kristen worked with Lauren's students, she found some who preferred to read in print and others who wished that all of their school reading was digital. She also realized that Lauren is doing her best with the technology available to her to help her students traverse all kinds of texts. When possible, Lauren, relying on the tenets of fair use, turns print reading digital by snapping pictures of the assigned pages and sending them to her students so they can read them on the subway. We believe that all teachers have many opportunities to do this same kind of work, regardless of the access to technology in their own classrooms.

While we admit that the majority of texts that students encounter in school are handed to them as assignments, or part of "required reading," we feel we can broaden the ways in which students find, discuss, and share texts, especially texts of their own choosing. We also see the need to help students make their reading practices transparent and connect those practices to other readers, who may influence the meaning they make from a text. Moreover, we see no reason to completely abandon print texts; instead, we can use digital tools and the principles of Connected Reading to enhance our experiences with those texts. In this chapter, we share examples of using digital tools to enhance print reading in order to create Connected Readers, focusing on how teachers might help students encounter, engage, and evaluate texts.

Encountering: Finding Texts from Real-World Readers

When Kristen was teaching high school, she asked her students to read independently, and she required one book per marking period beyond the assigned texts. Finding little value in a book report that was submitted for her eyes only, initially Kristen asked students to create index card book reviews that were tacked to a bulletin board in the room. She hoped the public display would encourage reading.

Her students dutifully completed the task in response to their own reading, but no one read the reviews and no one talked about them. No one was inspired by the reading of others to pick up a book. So Kristen changed course. She began to allow her students to create their own assessments, and she encouraged them to share their reading with others through this process. Knowing that her students instant messaged one another regularly outside of school, Kristen suggested that a group hold a discussion of their book via instant messaging (IM). They did, and independent reading instantaneously changed. Conversations that began online started trickling into the classroom, and titles that the teens enjoyed started being passed among peers.

Fast-forward a decade, and we see how digital tools can help to engage students with their reading, but even more important, the Internet offers an opportunity for teen readers to connect with other readers across the globe. Natalie's experience, described in the next section, demonstrates the power of connecting readers.

Going beyond a Book Report

Each year Natalie's seniors complete an independent reading project. They are required to select any novel on the school's approved list, read it thoroughly, and present an analysis to the class. Natalie saves this unit for last to keep her students engaged as they head toward graduation. In the past, however, her students struggled to maintain their commitment to their reading amidst their developing "senioritis," and Natalie found their presentations less than inspiring.

Given her interest in digital literacy, Natalie decided to try an alternate approach to the unit, one that would require students to use digital tools to share their reading. In lieu of the book report, she asked them to develop wiki pages that showcased their analyses and digital book trailers that advertised the book. Both of these compositions were housed on the school library's website and shared with younger students as they selected their summer reading books. Natalie reflects on the experience:

> For many students, the act of reading must be meaningful. The independent reading project provided my students with an opportunity to connect with other students and showcase what they were reading, helping them see not only the value of the task for themselves, but also the potential value for others. Having their wiki pages and digital trailers available for peers and younger students to peruse offered my students a unique publishing experience. My students demonstrated pride in their work, knowing that other students could refer to it.
>
> They also demonstrated a deeper connection with the material than when they were assigned essays or verbal reports. They knew no one was reading those essays but me, their teacher. The book trailer, however, allowed them to experiment with digital tools. Since so many of my students use social media, their digital trailers evolved organically. My students were more enthusiastic, and they were willing to share their work more openly. They seemed to realize through this project that despite their differences of opinions or personal preferences, they all spoke the same language through their digital trailers. The independent reading project bridged the gap between boys and girls, seniors and freshmen, sci-fi lovers and romantics. It gave each of my students a sense of empowerment, and that confidence spilled forth as a newfound interest in sharing.
>
> My students' participation in the independent reading project was more profound than in any other project; it created a rare opportunity for my students' work to serve a purpose beyond completion. Utilizing my students' work on their projects as a means to attract other potential readers' attention made the project meaningful to my own students, and also to those who may find it helpful in future independent reading selections. The value of this project was not only what my students learned from reading the text and creating the digital trailer, but also how my students connected with others, and the infinite possibilities surrounding those other students' experiences with my students' work. (Natalie, English teacher)

Nearly all of Natalie's seventy-five seniors read books in print form, yet they were able to share that reading with a broad audience using digital tools, and students like Leo, profiled in Chapter 4 as a reluctant reader, were excited to create these products. Even more exciting, however, is the opportunity that younger students now have as a result of this shared reading. With the wiki pages and digital trailers archived, students in years to come can see what others have read and select texts based on the recommendations of real readers, rather than from a list of books provided by the school. We are sure that many of you, as adult readers, have valued making connections with other real readers across time and space, and you know how powerful others' suggestions can be for your own reading choices. How then can you help your readers become more skilled at using digital tools to make these connections?

Tools to Connect Readers before and after Reading

Natalie chose wikis and digital book trailers to facilitate her students' postreading activities, but there are many tools available for finding and sharing reading. One of our study participants, Kelly, indicates that she often reads reviews on Goodreads before reading print books assigned by her teachers, and we know that Shelfari is another popular site where readers can read and post reviews. Connections that used to be made (or not) through book reports stapled to the bulletin board can now extend beyond the classroom, connecting print and digital lives.

As you consider the possibilities for how to transform book reports into more meaningful genres and experiences, we encourage you first to review Diana Mitchell's classic article from *English Journal*, "Fifty Alternatives to the Book Report" (1998). Think about what each of these unique genres—from a college application letter to a yearbook entry to a family history—might look like now, nearly two decades after this article first appeared. It is also worthwhile to think with your students about what new "alternatives" they might offer to the book report, based on the websites and apps they use *right now*. While it may be passé by the time this book is published, the winter of 2013–14 was characterized by the "selfie" photograph, most notably with Ellen DeGeneres at the Oscars. What if students were to take a selfie with their book but do so in a unique space or with clothing that represented the setting? Grade 5 teacher Katharine Hale from Abingdon Elementary School in Arlington, Virginia, has her students take pictures of what they are reading and share with the hashtag "readergrams" through their class Twitter account. The possibilities are endless.

In the next few sections, we provide more specific and detailed examples of how students can participate in print-based reading using digital tools. Although this list is not by any means exhaustive, we provide some ideas for moving beyond the book report, digitally, in order to connect readers.

Digital Literature Circles

Readers have gathered in groups to talk about books for, we imagine, as long as books have existed. A more recent version of communal reading has developed into school reading practice with Daniels's book *Literature Circles: Voice and Choice in*

Book Clubs and Reading Groups (2002). In their recent update to the practice, Hyler and Hicks (2014) describe the way in which students "create a wiki for their literature circles in order to engage in thoughtful conversations while reading the book and demonstrate their understanding and comprehension of the text they have chosen" (p. 114). In this sense, Hyler's students participate in "digital literature circles" built on the idea that each student takes an active role in a shared reading process. Roles include those popularized in Daniels's original book: discussion manager, summarizer, and connector, among others.

Sharing their work on a wiki page, students are able to collaboratively construct meaning from the text as each contributes his or her components to the page. These components could include quotations from the text, digital book talks in the form of a video, links to definitions of vocabulary words, images or comics created to visually represent the text, or many other creative expressions. For more information and examples, visit Hyler and Hicks's companion wiki page to their book: http://createcomposeconnect.wikispaces.com.

Digital Book Trailers

Digital book trailers, otherwise known as "digital book talks," are described as "short, two to three minute videos that introduce the basic story line and in which the story is re-enacted with similar artistic and creative decisions made by a movie director as to what parts of the story are presented in a film he or she is creating." This definition, from the Digital Booktalk website (www.digitalbooktalk.net), provides hints of the creative possibilities afforded by digital media as well as the narrative elements that can be portrayed in a digital book talk. Gunter and Kenny (2008) describe the purpose of the book talk as different from simply advertising the book in that it "has a dual obligation to remain true to the book's essence so that an informed decision to read the book can be made and to provide an appealing advanced organizer to ready the student for the upcoming reading experience" (n.p.).

Natalie's students uncovered a variety of tools to help them create digital book trailers, including Stupeflix, VoiceThread, Roxio PhotoShow, and YouTube. In addition to these and others your students might find, we recommend the following for your first jump into creating digital book talks:

- Early Elementary School—Little Bird Tales: http://littlebirdtales.com
- Upper Elementary School—Animoto: http://animoto.com/pro/education
- Middle and High School—WeVideo: www.wevideo.com/education

Online Book Reviews

Now a part of our everyday purchasing experiences on websites, product reviews—specifically book reviews—were once reserved for a special section of the newspaper. Now, however, anyone can publish a book review, and while some reviews are created to drive traffic to the products via social media ratings, others are legitimate. And while some are poorly written, others are written very well and might serve as good models for student writing. Understanding the genre of the online book review will help students think beyond merely summarizing a text.

For instance, on the Youth Voices website, middle and high school students compose thoughtful reviews of books on the "Booktalk" channel: http://youth voices.net/channel/37444. The Youth Voices website also offers "guides," or templates, for students to follow as they compose responses to both fiction (http://youthvoices.net/node/36253) and nonfiction books (http://youth voices.net/node/50368). Once teens understand the rhetorical considerations and practice writing quality reviews, they can post book reviews to social networks such as Goodreads (www.goodreads.com) or Shelfari (www.shelfari.com).

Multimedia Book Response

More recently, as digital writing tools have expanded in scope and digital writers are able to produce text across media and genres (Hicks, 2013), additional forms of response have become possible. For instance, teachers are now sharing examples of student book responses in the form of:

- Glogster interactive posters: http://edu.glogster.com
- Comics created in ToonDoo (www.toondoo.com) or Bitstrips (www.bitstripsforschools.com)
- Animated cartoons created with Digital Films: www.digitalfilms.com
- Video games created with Scratch (http://scratch.mit.edu) or Gamestar Mechanic (http://gamestarmechanic.com)
- "Augmented reality" videos created with an app such as Aurasma (www.aurasma.com), where users can scan the book cover with their smartphone to be taken to a digital book trailer or other form of review

The possibilities of multimedia book response are unlimited, and we encourage you to see what other teachers are doing in this area. These sources could be useful as you explore:

- Cool Tools for Schools: http://cooltoolsforschools.wikispaces.com
- Cool Apps for Schools: http://coolappsforschools.wikispaces.com
- 50+ Web Ways to Tell a Story wiki: http://50ways.wikispaces.com
- Crafting Digital Writing wiki: http://digitalwritingworkshop.wikispaces.com/Websites_And_Apps

- Connected Reading Companion wiki: http://connectedreading.wikispaces .com

A Note on Digital Citizenship

We understand that both moving instruction and assessment into online spaces where students have access to the work and thinking of others require additional strategies of "classroom" management. As Natalie discovered when she introduced the wiki to her seniors, some students did not respect the virtual space. Though it is beyond the scope of this book to focus on lessons related to digital citizenship and creating positive digital footprints, we believe this kind of work is necessary early in the year.

If the Internet is an extension of the physical classroom, then teens must understand the social rules of participation and be held accountable to those rules. Though acceptable use policies cover some of this work in relation to school policies, learning to be Connected Readers involves understanding the space in which readers connect. You can find resources for teaching digital citizenship at Common Sense Media (www.commonsensemedia.org), Digital Is (digitalis.nwp.org), and the Digital ID project (http://digital-id.wikispaces.com).

Two quick notes on the lesson plans in this chapter and the next. First, you will notice that we have granted permission for you to copy and use these lessons in your classroom. Second, we have chosen not to put in suggested "time frames" because we know that the length of the lesson will vary based on whether you are working with middle school or high school students; the access you have in your classroom to computers, tablets, or BYOD (bring your own device) options; and how much of the work you are willing to assign as homework. Therefore, we encourage you to use these lessons not as specific templates but as heuristics to begin thinking about how to teach digital reading to your students.

Engaging: Transforming Annotations of Print Text with Digital Tools

Close reading is all the rage, but as NCTE's policy research brief *Reading Instruction for All Students* reminds us, it is just one of many strategies for engaging deeply with a text. Before we begin our explanation of how we would turn print texts digital, it is important to reiterate the point that not every section of every text requires a close reading. Some experts recommend a close reading of only four or five passages in an entire novel or, alternatively, one close reading of a nonfiction article out of every four or five that you read. Fisher and Frey (2013) outline three questions for students to use as they engage in close reading:

- What does the text say?
- How does the text work?

- What does the text mean?

These are questions that all readers can ask themselves during any reading. But the process of reading and then rereading looking for details to support close and critical interpretation is not something we should subject students to every single time they pick up a book or encounter a new text. For this reason, we think it is acceptable to closely read only the text that we can capture in a picture taken with a mobile device.

Here we share two examples of teachers who combine close reading and Connected Reading practices to support all of their students in reading literature. Because we were fortunate to team-teach with these teachers—Jen and Dawn—we also offer our reflections on the lessons and a revised conception of the process using an example from *Alice's Adventures in Wonderland*.

Making Reading Not So "Secret" in *The Secret Life of Bees*

Jen, a ninth-grade teacher, had one more unit before the final exam, which included a district-mandated "commentary" essay. The commentary required students to read a complex text, annotate a passage, and analyze literary devices in relation to a theme. Jen had been scaffolding her students' close reading skills since the beginning of the year, and as a leader in technology integration in her school, which had just approved a BYOD policy, she was more than willing to experiment in this final unit as her students read *The Secret Life of Bees* (Kidd, 2002).

The books would be read in print form, but the students would have access to various devices in the classroom, as well as at home. Considering these technologies (print text, Chromebooks, iPads, iPhones, and Androids), Jen worked with Kristen to determine how to augment the students' print reading of *The Secret Life of Bees* with the use of digital tools. They decided to ask students to digitally annotate one passage by transferring their class notes to screen, to share the thinking behind their annotation via a screencast, and to comment on their peers' digital work. All of this work would serve as an assessment of their ability to read closely, as well as a rough draft for the unit commentary, which would be written at home.

Over the course of the three-week unit, Jen guided her students through whole-class discussion about the novel. Each student was assigned one of five specific passages that formed the basis of their analysis and discussion, and on their assigned days, students shared their close readings (in print) with the rest of the students, who dutifully marked up their own printed photocopies of the passage. As the unit assessment drew near, Kristen prepared an introduction to digital annotation and screencasting (see Figure 5.2), and she demonstrated how students could use their computers or handheld devices to do the same kinds of annotation they had been doing on their print copies of the text.

Figure 5.2. Digital annotation and screencasting lesson.

Digital Annotation and Screencasting Lesson

Standards

- CCSS.ELA-Literacy.CCRA.R.1. Read closely to determine what the text says explicitly and to make logical inferences from it; cite specific textual evidence when writing or speaking to support conclusions drawn from the text.
- CCSS.ELA-Literacy.CCRA.R.4. Interpret words and phrases as they are used in a text, including determining technical, connotative, and figurative meanings, and analyze how specific word choices shape meaning or tone.
- CCSS.ELA-Literacy.CCRA.R.10. Read and comprehend complex literary and informational texts independently and proficiently.

Rationale

To read and comprehend complex literary texts (R.10), students must be able to read closely, determining what the text says explicitly, and to cite specific textual evidence when speaking about the text (R.1). This work involves interpreting words and phrases and determining meanings (R.4). For digital texts, this work can be accomplished using digital tools.

Goals

Students will be able to use digital tools to annotate a passage and to reflect on their reading.

Formative Assessment

Individual screencast of close reading of assigned passage from *The Secret Life of Bees*

Materials

- Laptop with digital tools installed and projector
- Thinking about Reading handout (Figure 5.3)
- JPEG of *The Secret Life of Bees* passage

Lesson Plan

1. Have students answer the introductory questions on the handout and share responses with the class to arrive at appropriate definitions. Discuss why individuals might want to create screencasts or screenshots. What are the typical contexts in which students see these types of digital texts?
2. Ask students to consider how these digital tools might be useful in annotating texts and reflecting on their reading. Base this conversation in the knowledge they have gained about annotating print texts.
3. Share sample screencast that demonstrates digital annotation and reflection.
4. Model the annotation (with screencasting) with the whole class using the sample passage from *The Secret Life of Bees*.
5. Review the steps outlined on the handout and the resources suggested for completing the assignment. Extension/Differentiation: Note the tools for iPad. (These will not be demonstrated in class but will be noted for those students who want to learn them on their own.)
6. Have students respond to the reflection question and share their responses.

Figure 5.3. Handout on thinking about reading.

Thinking about Reading

How can I use digital tools to help me think about my reading? What other apps or websites do you know about that might be useful?

Overview

What is a screenshot?

How is a screencast different from a screenshot?

Annotating on the Computer

How do I annotate a passage from a novel?

To annotate on the computer:

1. Take a picture of your passage (or scan it) and transfer it to your computer. You can do this by taking the picture with your phone and emailing it to yourself. Don't forget to rotate the image if you need to do so before you send it.
2. Install the Chrome plug in for Awesome Screenshot.
3. Open the picture that you sent to your email. Click on the Awesome Screenshot extension so that you can annotate the text.
4. Open a new tab and start Screencast-o-matic. Begin recording. You can pause the recording by clicking the button in the lower left corner.
5. Switch back to the tab with the picture of your text, start the screencast recording, and begin annotating.
6. Save the recording by uploading to Youtube.

See Dr. Turner's sample at: http://youtu.be/f3Xhnvas52U

Notes

Materials Needed

To complete the screencast, you need:

- A picture or scan of your assigned passage from *Secret Life of Bees*

- A computer or iPad with a microphone

- An annotation program

- A screencasting program

Resources

For computer (demonstrated in class and video)

Screencast-o-matic

http://www.screencast-o-matic.com/

Awesome Screenshot

http://awesomescreenshot.com/

For Ipad (not demonstrated in class)

Educreations

http://www.educreations.com/

Skitch

http://evernote.com/skitch/

Some of the students found this task easy, and they quickly completed their screencasts. Others questioned why they had to "redo" the same annotation they had already done in print. Still others struggled with the technology, and both Jen and Kristen spent time helping students during lunch to complete the screencasts.

Overall, the lesson successfully introduced students to digital annotation and helped many to learn nuances of speaking publicly via a screencast. It also allowed students to comment on one another's thinking prior to the commentary essay. We realized, however, that waiting until the end of the unit to introduce the digital tools may have overwhelmed some students. In addition, the conversations that occurred during the seminar discussions existed only in the moment. Digital annotation allows those shared readings to live on the screen indefinitely. A more sustained approach to using the digital tools would make the print and digital experiences seamless, and it would also connect readers throughout the process in a way that leads naturally to the final assessment.

Identifying Motifs in *To Kill a Mockingbird*

Dawn sees great importance in helping her students learn to annotate a text in order to hone critical reading skills. She regularly uses sticky notes for annotation, and she was willing to experiment with digital tools to explore the possibilities of close reading. She and Troy worked together to design lessons for her ninth-grade students related to *To Kill a Mockingbird* (Lee, 1960). Dawn explains this work:

> During our reading of *To Kill a Mockingbird* by Harper Lee, I have always had students read closely to find specific motifs that appear in the text, including education and schooling, prejudice, gender roles (including analysis of femininity), truth and trust, coming of age, and, finally, courage and bravery. In the past, students have read to find passages that reflect these motifs and then they write the passage down in a two-column chart, noting the passage in one column and in the second column writing a response to the passage with explanation of how it relates to the motif.
>
> This chart, like a dialectic journal, focuses students' reading around common thematic ideas in a text for the purpose of careful reading; in so doing, it leads to conversations about the message of the novel. This year, when Troy collaborated with me, we invited students to capture passages as they read, either by writing down the passage, as students had done in the past, or taking digital pictures of a passage. This step offered opportunities for close reading, but invited them to use their smartphone, which made the task less onerous and much more natural for several students. With this simple adjustment to the assignment, I was welcomed with fewer groans from students about their task of recording a passage. Instead, their attention went to finding examples and engaging in the task.

Because this initial attempt at digital annotation occurred in the middle of their reading of the novel, Dawn's students had one weekend to complete this task, returning on Monday with their images and annotations. Since their work was to tie specific passages of the text to the broader motifs in the novel, Dawn already had them working in groups based on the motifs noted earlier. Also of note, Dawn's school uses Google Apps for Education, so her students were generally comfortable using Google Docs as a tool.

So on Monday, Troy taught a brief mini-lesson on how to create a group presentation, which included having each group member import his or her images from the text into the presentation. Both Troy and Dawn worked with students, individually and in groups, showing them how to use drawing tools and commenting features in Google Presentations (Figure 5.4). Here, Dawn reflects on that process:

> In a team devoted to focus on one of the motifs, students collaborated by uploading the figures of their passages and then responding to one another about how those passages related to the motifs. No longer did I have students working independently; rather, students were collaborating in a shared document. In the past, the classroom collaboration focused on discussion in class. With the use of a Google presentation, students could now see what each member of their group found for their passage, supporting the visual learner and clarifying much faster and more clearly if similar passages were highlighted or not, which then led to conversation about how each passage did or did not relate to the motif.
>
> Additionally, this process provided a focus for students in their work with motifs, narrowing their goals and prompting a careful reading that was a much more manageable opportunity to engage in close reading. Once students posted their passages, they responded to that passage, and to one another, by sharing their thinking and connections to the text, noting what specifically in the text made them think about the connection between the passage and the motif.

Figure 5.5 shows what one slide in one group's presentation looked like in its final form. On the left, the snapshot of page 247, Chapter 27, from the book appears with a purple rectangle highlighting the key passage. On the right, students have worked together to write an explanation of the passage, connecting their interpretation to the broader motif of "coming of age." What is not visible in this final slide are all the comments and notes that students shared in the process of composing the final presentation. Some groups used the comments feature in Google Presentations; others used the notes function to add their ideas and questions. Still other groups, when working synchronously, used the built-in Google chat feature to discuss their passages and connections to the broader motifs. Dawn summarizes and reflects on the experience:

Figure 5.4. Students annotating a screenshot using Google Presentations.

Figure 5.5. Sample slide from the "Coming of Age" motif presentation.

Example 3, Page 247

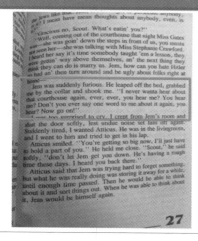

In this passage, Jem lashes out at Scout when she talks about her teacher at the courthouse. You can tell as he is very passionate about the case and fully understands what is going on in the town. At the beginning of the book, he might not have had this understanding or have even cared about what is going on. This shows that he has grown up. He is now old enough to know about segregation and have an opinion about it.

Close reading as a collaborative conversation was very rich throughout this work. At quick glance, this work didn't seem all that revolutionary to me. But when teased out to look at the opportunities for engagement and collaborative learning, this modification to the lesson offered a rich reading experience for my students. It also honored the various ways we read and can learn with digital tools. Collaboration through digital tools offers wonderful connected reading practices that I will continue to use in my classroom.

Again, it is important to note that this process began for Dawn's students in the middle of their whole-class reading of *To Kill a Mockingbird* and, over time, led to those collaborative conversations. Rather than keeping individual dialectal journals and then using those journals to spark class discussion, the groups worked together for a few weeks—from the midpoint of the book until the end—identifying key passages that dealt with their motif. They could, quite literally, see their group-mates' thinking unfold as they engaged with the second half of the novel. Near the end of the unit, students put the finishing touches to their slides and then delivered a final oral presentation to the entire class about their motif.

Revising Our Practice: From Print Texts to Digital Interpretation

We learned from our teen readers that, as Andrew said, "reading is supposed to be . . . connective," yet virtually none of them understood that digital tools can help them to connect during their reading. We also know that traditionally in school, which has been print-based, teachers have not been able to capture thinking across readers in a sustained way. Students possess their own copies of a text; they read and annotate those copies individually; and if they do work collaboratively to annotate, discussions are often lost to the wind. For these reasons, we created lessons to guide students in sharing their thinking, but we realize that this work cannot be a one-shot deal. To develop Connected Readers, we must sustain the practices of shared annotation and close reading.

Given this reflection, we recommend a combination of the work we did in both Jen's and Dawn's classrooms. This instruction would include regular, ongoing work in literature circles, where students bring important passages to discuss and the group determines the passages to annotate. Each student would add independent annotations to the passage that could contribute to further discussion within the group. At the end of the unit, we would ask students to create a presentation of their thinking about the novel using these shared annotations.

As we think about how to bring analog texts into a digital environment so students can annotate them—and share that annotation—there are a variety of tools and techniques that could be used in various combination with one another (see Figure 5.6 for examples of tools).

Figure 5.6. Tools for screencasting and screen capture.

	Screenshots	Screencasting
Browser-Based Tools	Awesome Screenshot http://awesomescreenshot.com Described on its website as a way to "capture the whole page or any portion, annotate it with rectangles, circles, arrows, lines and text, one-click upload to share," Awesome Screenshot lives up to its name. With plug-ins for Google Chrome, Firefox, and Safari, it is easy to use this tool within many Web browsers. Similar tools include: Snaggy: http://snag.gy qSnap: http://qsnapnet.com	Screenr www.screenr.com Like screenshots, screencasting allows you to capture any portion of your screen. However, it has the additional feature of being able to record this as a video, not just a still image. Screenr, while requiring the Java plug-in, is a free and easy tool that can be used across platforms and with any Web browser. Similar tools, each requiring Java, include: Screencast-O-Matic: www.screencast-o-matic.com ScreenCastle: http://screencastle.com
Downloadable Programs	Jing: www.techsmith.com/jing.html Skitch: https://evernote.com/skitch JShot: http://jshot.info Monosnap: http://monosnap.com	Jing: www.techsmith.com/jing.html QuickTime (Mac OSX): www.apple.com/quicktime CamStudio (Win): http://camstudio.org
iPad-Based Tools	Skitch Monosnap Picap	Educreations ScreenChomp TouchCast

We next look deeper into each step and its applications in the classroom. For these examples, we use Lewis Carroll's *Alice's Adventures in Wonderland* (1865) because it's available in the public domain and we didn't need to secure additional permission from the copyright holder to reprint the book. Please note, however, that under fair use guidelines of the US Copyright Act, you and your students have a wide degree of latitude in using copyrighted texts for educational purposes so long as they are used in a transformative manner. As Renee Hobbs argues in her book *Copyright Clarity: How Fair Use Supports Digital Learning* (2010), "Making reference to, using or quoting from the work of others is an example of fair use. . . . *Transformativeness* is the term emerging for the repurposing of copyrighted materials as part of the creative process" (p. 8). In other words, because your students would be using copyrighted language from an existing text in a way that was different from its original purpose and that also enhances academic understanding of the text, their use of the text is considered transformative. It is perfectly legal, as well as academically appropriate, for you to ask your students to take a picture of a page in a book and then annotate it in the ways we are describing.

For this particular example, we share Troy's annotations of "Down the Rabbit Hole" from the first chapter of *Alice's Adventures in Wonderland*. It occurs after Alice has shrunk and is unable to climb back onto the table. We describe here three basic steps (Figure 5.7), each of which can be accomplished using the tools mentioned earlier or others that you or your students might know. Troy used Skitch as the screen capture app to complete steps 1 and 2 before moving into Google Presentations for step 3. He describes his process:

> **Step 1:** I use my phone to snap a picture of an important part of the text using the Skitch app. This task is very easy since the app opens immediately to a camera view. I push the button and, voilà, the printed page from the book is now a digital image on my phone.
>
> **Step 2:** I add brief annotations with the tools present in the screen capture program (in this case Skitch). For students to demonstrate their engagement with the text, these brief annotations can be used to ask a question, make a connection, or engage in another during-reading strategy. Here I'm going to rely on Fisher and Frey's (2013) first question, "What does the text say?" I've typed a brief response: "Here, Alice is talking to herself in a scolding manner, much as a Victorian parent might do with his/her child." You can see my sample annotation in Figure 5.8. I must save and export the file. Using the Skitch app, I can generate a JPEG file and save it to my camera roll, then upload it to Google Drive.
>
> **Step 3:** I can share my annotation with others so that I can discuss the questions that Fisher and Frey offer: "How does the text work?" and "What does the text mean?"

We now step back from Troy's annotation to consider this last phase of the process. We can structure this activity of collaboration in many ways, and for this particular example, we will imagine that we are asking students to individually identify critical passages from the first chapter and to prepare to discuss them in relation to Lewis Carroll's perception of Victorian England. In this case, four students would work together to develop a collaborative Google Presentation. After sharing their individual screenshots, the group would collect one important passage from each person and create a slide that includes each of the original snapshots (with initial annotation) taken by each group member. The next task would be to look closely at each of the four passages, focusing on how the text works and what it means.

Students would use the commenting tool within Google Presentations to discuss their ideas, with each group member contributing comments in response to the others' annotations. We demonstrate this possibility in Figure 5.9. After this work is complete, the individuals responsible for the slide would summarize the group's thinking about the passage in the notes section below the slide. This work would become the basis for oral presentations of their close readings to the rest of the class.

Figure 5.7. Three steps for bringing analog texts into a digital environment.

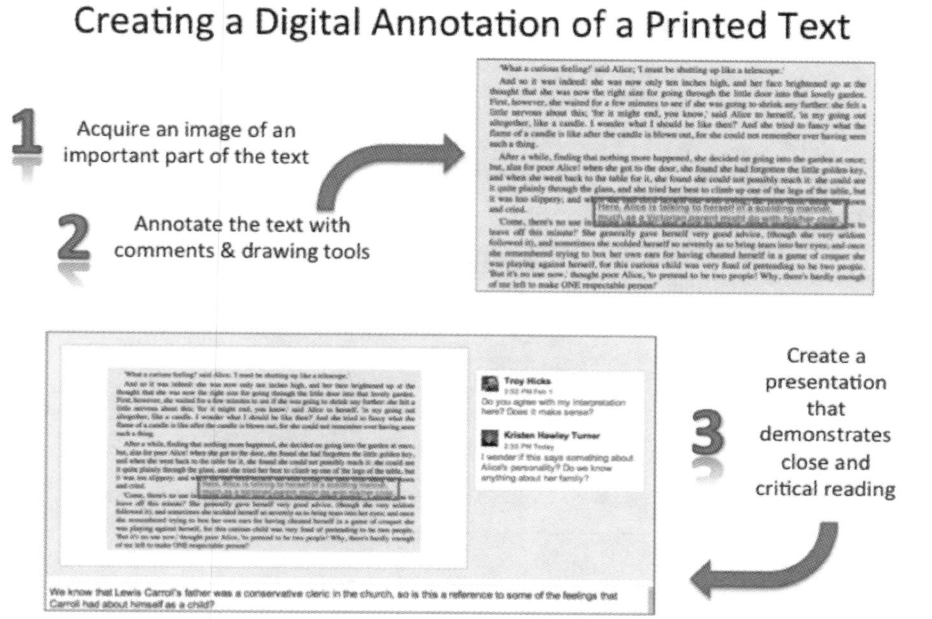

Creating a Digital Annotation of a Printed Text

1 Acquire an image of an important part of the text

2 Annotate the text with comments & drawing tools

3 Create a presentation that demonstrates close and critical reading

Figure 5.8. Initial annotation with Skitch focusing on what the text itself actually says.

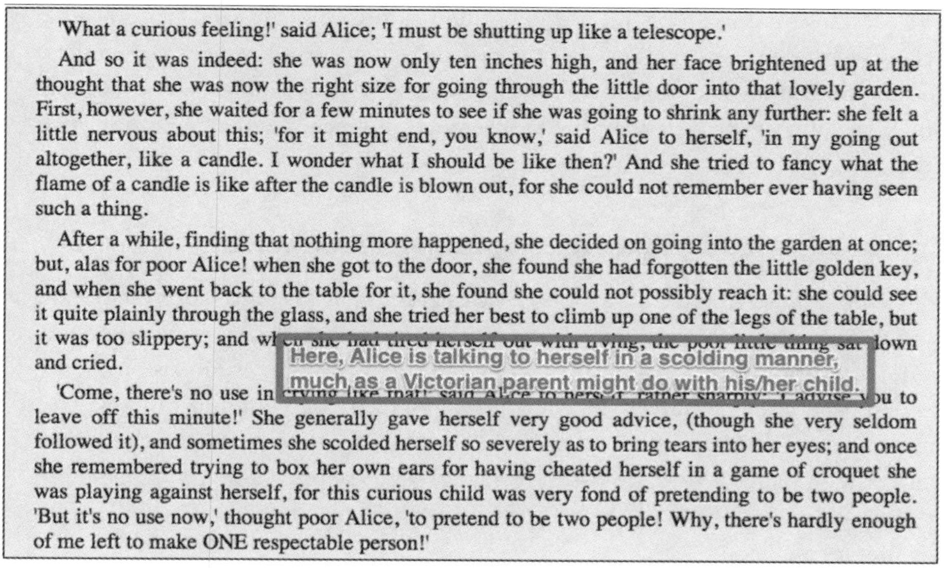

'What a curious feeling!' said Alice; 'I must be shutting up like a telescope.'

And so it was indeed: she was now only ten inches high, and her face brightened up at the thought that she was now the right size for going through the little door into that lovely garden. First, however, she waited for a few minutes to see if she was going to shrink any further: she felt a little nervous about this; 'for it might end, you know,' said Alice to herself, 'in my going out altogether, like a candle. I wonder what I should be like then?' And she tried to fancy what the flame of a candle is like after the candle is blown out, for she could not remember ever having seen such a thing.

After a while, finding that nothing more happened, she decided on going into the garden at once; but, alas for poor Alice! when she got to the door, she found she had forgotten the little golden key, and when she went back to the table for it, she found she could not possibly reach it: she could see it quite plainly through the glass, and she tried her best to climb up one of the legs of the table, but it was too slippery; and when she had tired herself out with trying, the poor little thing sat down and cried.

Here, Alice is talking to herself in a scolding manner, much as a Victorian parent might do with his/her child.

'Come, there's no use in crying like that!' said Alice to herself, rather sharply; 'I advise you to leave off this minute!' She generally gave herself very good advice, (though she very seldom followed it), and sometimes she scolded herself so severely as to bring tears into her eyes; and once she remembered trying to box her own ears for having cheated herself in a game of croquet she was playing against herself, for this curious child was very fond of pretending to be two people. 'But it's no use now,' thought poor Alice, 'to pretend to be two people! Why, there's hardly enough of me left to make ONE respectable person!'

Figure 5.9. Additional annotations on the text after importing to Google Presentations.

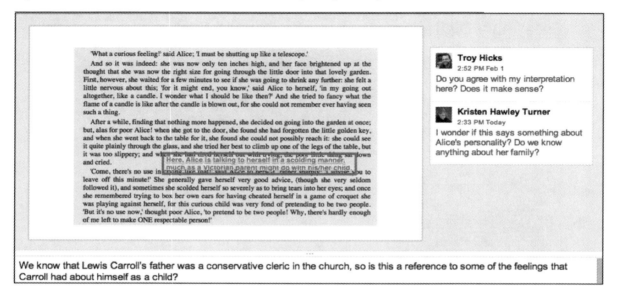

Google provides many free tools that facilitate collaboration and sharing, but we could ask students to do this work in a variety of ways. They might develop a short screencast in which they think aloud about what the text says, how it works, and what it means, or the group could work together to develop a VoiceThread, which allows them to literally offer comments to one another by typing or talking. We see value in these tools for documenting reading strategies and critical thinking related to the text. No matter what the task or tool, we would encourage students to stay focused on a particular section of the text, moving from the first question about the literal words on the page to inference and meaning making, rather than trying to closely read an entire chapter.

Evaluating: Finding and Creating Value in Print Texts

Evaluating can be defined as "judging," as in grading or keeping score. Yet it also means "assigning value" to something, a value that may be more personal in nature and not meant purely for assessment. In Connected Reading, we focus on the second part of the definition. Outside of school, teens are reading a lot. They read many kinds of texts, and they evaluate the worth of those texts as they choose to engage with them or to share them. In school they are often asked to judge their reading, not on the basis of a text's perceived value but on a set of universal criteria for literary analysis.

Rather than asking students to be literary critics who judge every text they read, we want to ask them to consider the value of any given text, a value they can bring to themselves and to others.

Embedded in these activities are questions of how students encounter and engage with texts. We provide here a series of questions for you to consider as you plan your reading instruction (of print texts) with this idea of evaluation in mind:

- How often do you assign your students the texts they will read for your class?

- When reading independently, do they read to fulfill required minutes or to meet their own intentions?

- How do you invite students to decide what to do with a text once finished, for instance by asking questions such as, "Do I want to share this text?" and "If so, how and when do I share it?" Do they have an audience beyond the classroom with whom they can share their reading?

- In what ways do students have the choice to engage with a text or to abandon it? If they *must* read a text that they do not immediately find valuable, how do you help them bring value to it?

- Connected Readers make choices about when and how they enter conversations—or purposefully avoid them—about texts. In what ways do your students get these kinds of choices in your classroom?

These questions may prompt subtle changes in your teaching that will shift adolescents from the role of literary critic to Connected Reader. In many instances, this shift can be accomplished by recasting questions about reading. For instance, instead of asking students to determine the literary merit of a plot—whether it is good or bad—we can ask them to articulate what they have learned about plot from reading a given story. In other words, how does this particular book bring value to a larger conversation about narratives?

Convincing a reluctant teen reader of the merit of canonical literature is a difficult job, and we think it is made more challenging when we ask them to be judges of works they do not find inherently valuable. Instead, we hope to help them see value by relating required reading to their own immediate purposes and their overarching intentions as readers. In this way, they can begin to evaluate texts in a new light, followed by more opportunities for critical and creative response using digital tools.

Recap: Encountering, Engaging, and Evaluating

Throughout this chapter, we provide a number of strategies by which students can encounter, engage, and evaluate print-based texts using digital tools. This is more than a novelty. This is more than just an attempt to "meet the needs" of "digital natives." Instead, our goal is to help students think carefully, critically, and deeply

about what and how they read. A final example from Lauren, shared months after
Kristen's original visit to her classroom, highlights the substantive changes that
have occurred in her teaching as she considers this approach.

Lauren's classroom is a print-based one, as evidenced by the notes on the
chalkboard in Figure 5.10. But this photo also demonstrates that Lauren's students
use digital tools to engage with their reading. They produced this list while working on public service announcements as a response to their reading of *Fist, Knife,
Stick, Gun* (Canada, 2010). Lauren, whose students are required to leave their
phones at the security desk, went to collect their phones and brought them to class
for the day. She watched one of her struggling readers (who happens to have ELL
and special ed classifications) edit video and publish his group's PSA before the
end of class. In turn, Lauren shared the video with Kristen, who was able to see the
group's work and to respond to their thinking despite the fact that she was not a
part of the class.

Figure 5.10. List of digital tools created by Lauren's students as they recorded and edited
PSAs.

This kind of work is possible when we consider how we can turn print reading digital in order to connect readers. When we read the "Implications for Instructional Policy" section in *Reading Instruction for* All *Students* with a view of evaluation as "value-bringing," we see opportunities to develop the practices of teen readers. As described in this chapter, we see many chances to develop Connected Readers even when we use print-based texts. In the next chapter, we add to that, looking at options for doing this same work with digital texts.

**Chapter
Six**

Working with Digital Texts and Digital Tools

I n the last chapter, we discussed ways to develop Connected Readers even if you mostly have access to print texts. In this chapter, we look to the possibilities of connecting readers through digital texts.

As our survey results show, and the profiles of adolescent read-ers also highlight, many students are already using digital devices to read what interests them. Inherently, this type of reading is connected, but as many of the students note, digital reading can quickly lead to distraction. How can we help students learn to move past that distraction when they read digitally? How can we help teen readers work diligently to make meaning from what they read and to share their thinking with others?

We are still asking students to encounter, engage with, and evaluate all kinds of texts—print and digital—but we recognize that the digital ones do offer some unique affordances. It's much faster, for instance, to copy, paste, and tweet out a great quote from an ebook, or to forward an online article via email, than it is to snap a picture of a print text, annotate it, upload it, and so on. In practice, digital texts equate to quicker connections.

During the writing of this book, we met many individuals who inspired our thinking. Most of these connections came through Twitter, and we were particularly impressed with one teacher we met during an #nctechat. Rebekah O. is working to redefine reading in her classroom, and she reflects on her path to change:

> Eighteen months ago, I was not a digital reader. In fact, had you suggested that I delve into the world of digital reading, I might have rolled my eyes and self-righteously told you that I prefer my reading on paper, *thankyouverymuch*. I refused to turn on the Kindle I was given as a Christmas gift. Twitter seemed like a burden to someone who was trying to quietly slip off Facebook without her family noticing. Beyond casual blog-following, digital reading seemed like just one more thing to do that would consume my time without adding meaning.
>
> And then something shifted. A colleague told me about all of the other teachers "like us" that were on Twitter. She encouraged me to wade into the Twitterverse to meet them. I remained hesitant, though, until I attended NCTE and saw my pen-and-notepad grossly outmatched by tablets and iPhones. I wanted to know what *these* colleagues were saying; I wanted to join *that* conversation. I began to realize that my reading-on-paper wouldn't be enough to connect with the world any longer.
>
> Reading has always been a medium of connection. Through books, readers are connected to ideas, to distant places, to the author, to vibrant characters, to new visions and understandings of themselves. But this isn't the whole story anymore. If the book connects readers internally, digital reading connects readers externally. I have become connected to a dynamic and inspiring world informed by my personal passions through my digital reading. I want the same for my students.

Rebekah is a Connected Reader and she wants the same for her students. For us this is a powerful testimony for changing what we do in the classroom.

Thus, this chapter presents a variety of instructional ideas that help us make the shift from traditional, print-based strategies for reading to adopting a more proactive stance toward digital texts. And here, when we say "digital texts," we do in fact mean born-digital texts, not just the PDF versions of texts meant for print that we discussed in the last chapter. Traditionally, comprehension strategies have focused on annotating, responding/discussing, analyzing, and evaluating words on paper, and it is possible for us to share tools that will simply substitute what we have always done with a fancy tool that does essentially the same thing for born-digital texts.

Indeed, using a new app or website for its own sake is not the essence of Connected Reading. Instead of simply extending our existing instructional practices to digital texts, we encourage you to think about how we might teach reading differently by redefining what we ask students to do as readers. In short, we do not want to substitute a tablet-based ebook for a print novel or ask students to read a current events article online rather than in the newspaper. Digital texts *function differently* than print texts, and we hope you will think about how these differences can be

Remember that all links and handouts are located on the companion wiki. Scan this QR code or go to http://connectedreading.wikispaces.com to access Chapter 6 materials.

productive and useful in connecting readers to one another in order to make meaning. We believe this work requires mindfulness, and we provide first an introductory lesson that engages adolescent readers in reflection on their own reading habits, followed by additional lessons and ideas for engaging readers in digital texts.

Reflecting on Reading: Seeing Ourselves as Digital Readers

The questions "Who am I as a writer?" and "Who am I as a reader?" have been asked of students since Donald Graves, Lucy Calkins, and Nancie Atwell introduced English teachers to workshop approaches in the 1980s. Troy has since argued that the question of writing identity must transcend a focus solely on print texts and that writers must consider the affordances of digital writing in defining their literate identities (Hicks, 2009, 2013; National Writing Project, 2010). In much the same manner as we have given agency to writers, we believe that readers also have a digital identity and must own their practices of digital reading. The lesson outlined in Figure 6.1 asks students to reflect on that identity in an attempt to answer the question, "Who am I as a (digital) reader?"

We were fortunate to conduct this lesson in many of the classes we visited, and we were inspired to see other teachers adapting it to their own contexts. Kaitlyn expanded the lesson in two areas that we think highlight the connectedness of readers in her classroom. First, she asked her students to examine the data generated by the survey using a "Looking at Data" protocol that she and her colleagues use regularly to reflect on student performance. Using this protocol helped her students to stay "grounded in evidence" rather than allowing their personal opinions to dominate discussion.

After small groups examined the data, she asked the whole class to set goals for their "reading culture" before turning to their own individualized goals. These activities helped to create a community of digital readers while at the same time honoring the individual practices of the students.

Kaitlyn noted the importance of this reflective activity for both her and her students:

> I believe one of the most surprising and interesting lessons my students learned from this experience is how to be cognizant of how they define literacy and what they see as "gathering information." Many of my students initially reflected that they never use digital resources to read. But upon consideration, it became clear that it was their interpretation of "reading" that caused them to ignore the many channels of digital resources they read on daily. This was very important for students because as they broaden their definition of literacy, they are able to be more critical in their reading lives.

This element of being "critical" begins with awareness of the texts, contexts, and attributes that influence reader choices. Through mindfulness, students can develop the practices of Connected Readers.

Figure 6.1. Lesson plan focused on the question "Who am I as a (digital) reader?"

"Who am I as a digital reader?"

Standards

- CCSS.ELA-Literacy.CCRA.R.7. Integrate and evaluate content presented in diverse media and formats, including visually and quantitatively, as well as in words.
- CCSS.ELA-Literacy.CCRA.R.10. Read and comprehend complex literary and informational texts independently and proficiently.

Rationale

To read and comprehend various kinds of texts (R.10), which include texts of diverse media (R.7), students must understand the nature of texts and consider how reading on devices differs from reading in print forms. This kind of understanding is best developed through reflection on practice, and this introduction to "What is reading?" begins with such reflection before turning to critical examination of various kinds of texts in order to compare and contrast print and digital reading.

Goals

- Students will compare and contrast print and digital texts and the reading processes associated with those texts.
- Students will reflect on their own reading practices and abilities, identifying strengths and weaknesses in both print and digital reading.

Formative Assessment

- Students will develop their own "digital reading goals" for academic and personal reading. See the suggested chart outline for this assessment below.

Materials

- Digital Reading Survey
- Computers or e-devices (if doing the survey in class)
- Student notebooks/paper/e-devices for reflective writing

Lesson Plan

Before the lesson, create a copy of the Digital Reading Survey (instructions for doing so are on our wiki: https://connectedreading.wikispaces.com).

1. Writing prompt/opening discussion. Ask students to think through the ways they read each day—any time they must make meaning from words. A prompt could be:

   From the moment we wake up until our heads hit the pillow again at night, our lives are full of reading. Think of as many times and places during the day that you read as you can. That is, quite literally, when must you make meaning from words from notes, status updates, signs, books, websites, or other sources? For each one, describe how this kind of reading helps you through your day.

2. Transition to the customized Digital Reading Survey. You can share the link on your class webpage. The form will aggregate the responses for the class. (The survey can be completed in class simultaneously or for homework individually.)

3. After completing the survey (or at the beginning of the class discussion), students write a brief reflection focused on "what I realized about myself as a reader as I answered the survey questions." Compare this reflection to their initial writing. What was the same? What was different? What was surprising?

continued on next page

Figure 6.1. Continued

4. Share the aggregate survey data with the class. (You can share visually via electronic display but might also verbally read the results to the class. Alternatively, you can ask students to read the results individually. See our screencast on the Connected Reading wiki for instructions.) As they are reviewing the results, students individually write down two things they find interesting about the data.

5. In small groups, the students share their points of interest and discuss what the data might *mean*. What does this say about me as a reader compared to my friends? What does it say about us overall as readers?

6. Each group shares one interpretation of the data with the class and provides a brief summary of the small-group conversation about that interpretation. After all groups have shared, facilitate a large-group conversation about what the students have discovered about themselves as readers, as well as the group as readers. This conversation might also focus on individual questions or sections in the survey. For example, you might choose to focus on how students answered the "out of school" reading questions in order to promote reflection and sharing of individual practices, or you might choose to focus on the "inside of school" questions to hone in on strategies for reading academically.

7. Students write "digital reading goals" for themselves. They might organize these goals in terms of "reading for school" and "reading for me." One possible format for writing the goals could look like this:

My Digital Reading Goals	Personal Goals	Academic Goals
When reading on the Web,	I will . . .	I will . . .
When reading digital books,	I will . . .	I will . . .
When reading on social networks,	I will . . .	I will . . .

Permission is granted for classroom use.

Receiving, Surfing, and Stumbling upon Digital Texts

In Chapter 2, we highlighted our own reading practices and the fact that *where* we read is closely tied to *when* we read. As we look to the variety of tools available for mobile devices as well as through stand-alone websites, we must become aware of the opportunities for our students to engage in a variety of digital texts, including short-, mid-, and long-forms. We know that students can access major news websites, personal blogs, and a variety of other sources using "push" technology; rather than actively searching to find resources, readers can have new, relevant material delivered directly to them from sources that push texts to potential users via pop-up alerts, emails, or a constantly refreshing homepage. To help students be mindful in these curating practices, we recommend that teachers create assignments that ask students to engage with RSS or other organizational tools. For example, in *The Digital Writing Workshop* (2009), Troy suggested that students engage in sustained silent reading (SSR) with RSS. We reintroduce that idea here in Figure 6.2 with a variety of tools that might help in the process.

Figure 6.2. Lesson plan on using RSS to fuel reading.

Using RSS to Fuel Your Reading

Standards

- CCSS.ELA-Literacy.CCRA.R.6. Assess how point of view or purpose shapes the content and style of a text.
- CCSS.ELA-Literacy.CCRA.R.9. Analyze how two or more texts address similar themes or topics in order to build knowledge or to compare the approaches the authors take.
- CCSS.ELA-Literacy.CCRA.R.10. Read and comprehend complex literary and informational texts independently and proficiently.

Rationale

To read and comprehend various kinds of texts (R.10), which include texts created by a variety of authors for numerous purposes and audiences (R.6 and R.9), students must seek out a variety of perspectives from the news media and blogs. RSS, a technology that pushes content out from websites to a user, is one tool that students can use to gather these various perspectives on a particular topic. Also, becoming a proficient reader of nonfiction text requires repeated exposure to disciplinary vocabulary over time, a practice that regular RSS reading can support.

Goals

- Students will demonstrate their ability to find and organize RSS feeds to make their own custom newsmagazine.
- Students will identify both personal and academic topics of interest, creating a customized search to load in their RSS reader.

Formative Assessment

- Students will set up their Feedly homepage for academic and personal reading, reflecting on the purposes for each type of news feed he or she includes. See the suggested outline for this assessment below.

Materials

- Access to Feedly.com and/or the Feedly app
- Print or digital version of the "Use RSS to Fuel Your Reading" handout: http://bit.ly/rssfuel
- Computers or e-devices (if doing the survey in class)
- Student notebooks/paper/e-devices for reflective writing

Lesson Plan

Before the lesson, you will need to confirm that all students have a Google account.

1. Show students the video "RSS in Plain English": www.commoncraft.com/video/rss.
2. Once completed, ask students to consider how news websites and blogs "push" out their content both to their homepages and to smartphone apps. Refer to the figures in Chapter 2 showing how the same content can appear through multiple sources but may look slightly different.
3. Pass out or ask students to link to the "Use RSS to Fuel Your Reading" handout and read the first two sections about Feedly. Using the website (Feedly.com) or the app, ask students to log in to Feedly with their Google accounts.
4. Invite students to navigate through the sections of Feedly and to find three feeds they are interested in. Subscribe to those feeds using the "+" button and also categorize those feeds. Allow students adequate time to find their feeds and, if they have completed the task, invite them to identify a few more of interest.

continued on next page

Figure 6.2. Continued

5. Ask students to load CNN.com in a Web browser. Using the handout, have them navigate to CNN's list of RSS feeds and manually subscribe to one of their choice.
6. Invite students to search the Web for additional RSS feeds using Instant RSS Search or RSSMicro. Alternatively, you can invite students to search Technorati for blogs related to relevant topics and get the RSS feed from those blogs: http://technorati.com.
7. Finally, introduce the Google Alerts page and ask students to generate a feed about a pertinent topic.

Creating My Reading List with Feedly

Our goal for creating a custom reading experience with Feedly is for both your personal reading and academic purposes. Based on the feeds that you have initially put in your Feedly, describe what you hope to read, learn, and enjoy. I've started the CNN one as an example:

Feed	Personal/ Academic	What I hope to read about and learn from this feed
CNN.com	Academic	Because we are studying US politics in social studies, I feel that this will be a reliable source of information for me.

A slight adaptation of this lesson would be to use the social reading platforms mentioned in Chapter 2: Flipboard, Pulse, Zite. These social reading platforms work by pulling in content from various websites and displaying it in a magazine-style format through the app. Along with the headline, the first few lines of the news story will often be displayed, as will embedded pictures. News can be taken directly from major sites such as CNN.com and can be searched and added with keywords or hash tags. Additionally, a customized Google Alert can be added.

Finally, a few reflections from Jenn, who shared this lesson with her students during Troy's visit to her classroom:

> The students were very excited about the possibilities of the RSS feed and Feedly. . . . Every student found something they could add to their feed, and many of the students were quite excited about the possibilities. As soon as our students have access to 1:1 technology, I can imagine ways in which we can incorporate regular use of their Feedly accounts. For example, my ninth graders and I are working on multigenre writing projects. I have been searching for examples of writing that we can break

down and explore and use as models. We are going in the computer lab tomorrow, so I am going to recommend that they access their Feedly accounts and use their topic as a search category. I imagine it will broaden their searches and hope that they can then submit examples of interesting writing. I think there are other ways that I could help support the students' regular use of RSS feeds. They just need regular access and a little encouragement. I suspect once they have that, they'll be off and running. They were clearly excited to investigate their own interests.

Searching for Digital Texts: Popping the Filter Bubble

While not a formal part of our study, the following question often received a one-word answer: when you sit down at your computer and open up an Internet browser, what is the first thing you do? You can probably guess the response: Google.

For nearly every student we talked to, the idea that they go to Google, and to a lesser extent Yahoo or Bing, permeated our discussions of how students actively seek out digital texts. A few also describe how their homepages may be set to Yahoo News or some other portal. Yet for the most part, students access the Internet assuming that it is a blank slate and that their search will yield only the best results. Sadly, this is not the case.

Many journalists and tech bloggers have outlined the ways in which search engines function, oftentimes in ways completely invisible to the user. For instance, whether you are logged in or not, Google uses a variety of data points to customize your search. While this may be good for marketing, it is not necessarily good for the free flow of information on the Internet. In his book *The Filter Bubble: What the Internet Is Hiding from You*, Eli Pariser (2011) outlines the perils associated with being confined to "an Internet of one." Specifically, he discusses how search algorithms may include or exclude particular results based on your previous Web searches, what you identified about yourself in your account profile, the particular location you are at when making the search, and a variety of other factors. The idea of an open, democratic Web has been replaced by search functions that are completely customized to you and, (not so) coincidentally, the advertising that the search engine wants to sell you.

To help students understand the inherent "filter bubble" in this process, we designed a lesson that focuses specifically on active searching for texts. To do so, we first watched Pariser's TED talk and then modeled a number of searches. For instance, with one teacher in Michigan, Troy used her computer to do a search for "tigers." On the first page of search results from Google, the top few hits before scrolling down were all related to the Detroit Major League Baseball team. Only after scrolling "below the fold," to use the old newspaper parlance, did images of actual tigers begin to appear. However, when switching to a variety of alternative search engines, some interesting results emerged (see Figures 6.3–6.6).

Figure 6.3. Troy's search for "tigers" on Google (based in Michigan).

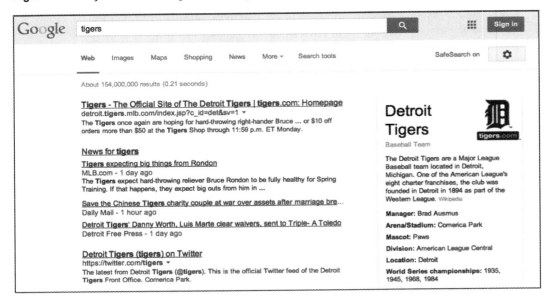

Figure 6.4. Kristen's search for "tigers" on Google (based in New Jersey).

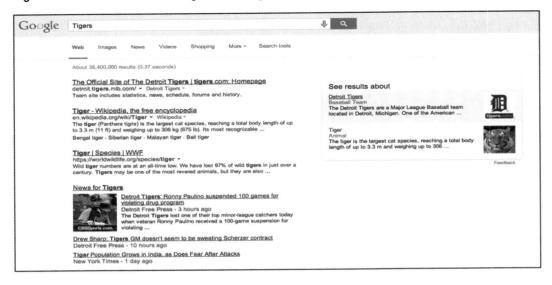

Figure 6.5. Search for "tigers" on DuckDuckGo.

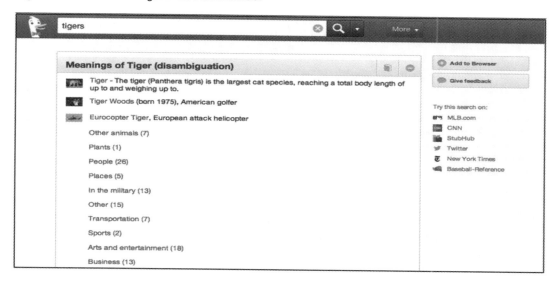

Figure 6.6. Search for "tigers" on Blekko.

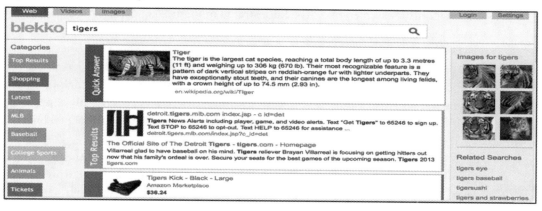

In Figure 6.3, the results for "tigers" yields a variety of information about the Detroit Tigers baseball team. Although there is one news story from *The Daily Mail*, the rest of the links and images are related to the team. Just below the fold, or where you would need to scroll past the first view search results, the Wikipedia entry for "Tiger" appears, followed a few links later by a link to the World Wildlife Fund website. Granted, Google did provide the option in its automatic search feature to search for the word *tiger* alone. Still, the preponderance of links related to the baseball team, when done as a search from a computer in Michigan, demonstrates one of the ways that Google's search algorithms customize results. This effect is even more apparent when comparing Troy's search to Kristen's search—from northern New Jersey, a decidedly Mets/Yankees area—shown in Figure 6.4. Only one hit for the Tigers baseball team before the engine delivered content related to animals.

In Figure 6.5, a different search engine, DuckDuckGo, immediately provides the user with various meanings of the word *tigers.* While the logo for MLB.com and Baseball-Reference appear on the side, DuckDuckGo does not, by default, assume much of anything in our search for the word "*tigers.*" After we click on the term from the disambiguation, a new link goes to yet another page of search results. When we click the minus sign at the end of the gray bar for "Meanings of Tiger," a variety of results appear in the top four hits, one to a sponsored link, the second to the official Major League Baseball website, the third to National Geographic Kids, and the fourth to the World Wildlife Fund. Describing itself as a search engine that protects your privacy and allows you to search anonymously, DuckDuckGo ostensibly provides results that are based less on your own search history and what you tend to like on the Internet and more on actual measures of currency and relevancy.

Another search engine worth exploring is Blekko, which describes itself as a categorical search engine. As demonstrated in Figure 6.6, Blekko's search result for "tigers" yields a variety of stories across different categories, including Quick Answer, Top Results, and Latest across the top, as well as other categories related to baseball and sports beneath. Each of these categories can be expanded to show more links within the heading. This type of categorical search can be helpful in the same way that DuckDuckGo provides disambiguation. It is also visually appealing in the sense that related images, sometimes just as informative as the actual links and snippets from the websites, show up alongside the search results.

There are a number of other search engines that students can use, and one lesson we have tried is to ask students to perform a search on the same word or phrase across multiple search engines, comparing the domain names of the top three results. Again, we've embedded this lesson in a broader conversation about how and why students choose to read particular online texts, as well as how they come to find those texts. In this work, we also talk about general search strategies, such as Boolean operators and the fact that searches should not be stated in the form of a question. The lesson in Figure 6.7 helps open up this conversation with your students.

Figure 6.7. Lesson plan comparing results from searches using multiple search engines.

Popping the Filter Bubble

Standards

- CCSS.ELA-Literacy.CCRA.R.5. Analyze the structure of texts, including how specific sentences, paragraphs, and larger portions of the text (e.g., a section, chapter, scene, or stanza) relate to each other and the whole.
- CCSS.ELA-Literacy.CCRA.R.7. Integrate and evaluate content presented in diverse media and formats, including visually and quantitatively, as well as in words.
- CCSS.ELA-Literacy.CCRA.R.10. Read and comprehend complex literary and informational texts independently and proficiently.

Rationale

To read and comprehend various kinds of texts (R.10), which include texts of diverse media (R.7), students must be able to make good choices about what they read online, beginning with how they find such texts. Because search engines often present a summary or the first few sentences from a website, it is important for students to be able to read those smaller sections and make informed inferences about the quality of those links (R.5). This lesson demonstrates the differences between various search engines and how their results are displayed, leading to questions about both how and why to conduct searches with various tools.

Goals

- Students will use multiple search engines to compare and contrast the top three results for two search terms.
- Students will reflect on their own Web searching practices, identifying ways they might change their search processes in the future.

Formative Assessment

- Students will complete the comparison of multiple search engines and reflect on their experiences. See the suggested outline for this assessment below.

Materials

- "Popping Our Online Filter Bubbles" handout—print or digital
- Eli Pariser's 2011 TED talk: www.ted.com/talks/eli_pariser_beware_online_filter_bubbles.html
- Computers or e-devices
- Student notebooks/paper/e-devices for reflective writing

Lesson Plan

1. Writing prompt/opening discussion. Ask students to think about how they find texts to read online. One-word answers may ensue, such as Google, Yahoo, or Bing. Remind them of other Connected Reading practices in which they may also "encounter" a text besides searching: receiving, surfing, and stumbling.
2. Play Eli Pariser's 2011 TED talk. If you are short on time, you might want to pause the video at about the six-minute mark (after he shows the slide for "information junkfood").
3. Invite students to respond to the idea of what a "filter bubble" is and what it means by doing a quick-write on their handout. They may then "turn and talk" to one another, or you might initiate a brief whole-class discussion.
4. Using Google, DuckDuckGo, and Blekko, demonstrate a search for a common term and how the search results vary across different engines. (You may want to do a search of two or three different terms if time allows.) It is

continued on next page

Figure 6.7. Continued

important that students understand that searching in the form of a question will not yield the same results as using a single term or one with a Boolean operator such as "and," "or," or "not."

5. Invite students to search for two separate terms on their own and to complete the handout as they search. If writing down answers on a print version of the handout, ask them to retrieve just the top-level domain (e.g., Wikipedia.org). If using the digital handout, have them copy and paste the entire URL.

6. Lead a brief class discussion and ask students to share their search results. Note similarities and differences in how search terms yielded results.

   a. What did you find similar or different in the results for your search terms in these different search engines compared to using Google, Yahoo, or Bing?

   b. How does the way that these search results show up affect the way you might choose to click on and eventually read these websites?

   c. How does the placement of advertisements affect the search results on these various sites?

7. Ask students to write a brief reflection on their handout using the writing prompts provided.

To extend this lesson, given adequate time, you might also invite students to explore blog search engines such as Technorati or Google Blog Search. Using these tools will show results only from blogs and not major websites. Work with students to discuss the difference between a corporate or organizational website and the work of an individual blogger, especially in reference to bias and fact versus opinion.

Understanding how search engines function remains one of the most important aspects of encountering texts, especially when one student's search results differ from another's. After Troy's visit to Jeremy's classroom, they talked about how students must understand that much of what they will ultimately read online is a function of how they begin this search process.

> With all of the new information that was being given to my students, I thought they were going to feel overwhelmed and confused. However, they weren't. . . . I saw two sections of seventh graders completely engaged in what was being taught to them and what they were being asked to do. One of the most compelling aspects that was revealed was that my students had a hard time not asking a question when they were trying to do a search on the Internet. It is something I am going to have to keep encouraging them to work on when we use the Internet for class projects. In addition, I was just as intrigued with the idea of filter bubbles as the students were. It was a classic case of the teacher learning beside the students. Because I was reminded of using search engines such as Blekko and DuckDuckGo, I will encourage my students to think outside of the "Google" box and expand their searches to these other sites.

Taken in combination with the other digital reading strategies in this chapter, effective search technique can give our students access to a wider variety of digital texts.

Deciding on a (Less Distracting) Path with Digital Texts

In *The Art of Slow Reading* (2012), Tom Newkirk argues that readers must slow down and attend deeply to their reading in order to engage with it. We believe that digital texts are worthy of this same time and attention too, yet we know from our student participants that they read quickly, skimming and scanning short-forms regularly. From the moment an individual lands on a webpage, he or she has many decisions to make. It is important for teens to recognize these decision points and to slow down, thinking through their choices and whether reading, saving, or abandoning a given text will be valuable. The lesson idea "Decisions, Decisions, Decisions" (Figure 6.8) asks students to reflect on their decisions and to evaluate their purposes and intentions in their reading choices. It also encourages consideration of distractions during this process. By focusing on this first step in a reader's engagement with a text, we can begin to develop mindfulness in our adolescent readers.

Curating Digital Texts

Natalie's seniors sat stone-faced and silent as she introduced the lesson. She said, "I'm going to give you a tool to help you gather your research." They watched as she demonstrated Citelighter (www.citelighter.com), a tool that allows a reader to capture information from the Internet, import it and the bibliographic information into the platform, comment on the captured quotation, and organize the information before exporting it into a document. As she exported her quotations into a Word document, Natalie explained, "And here they are . . . the quotes, the comments on the quotes, and if you scroll down, the works cited." The atmosphere in the room shifted palpably. Responses included: "Wow," "Cool," and "That's awesome," all high praise from teens.

Natalie's students were impressed by the capabilities of the tool, and as Kristen chatted with them while they worked independently, it became clear that they found value in the way Citelighter helped them to curate digital texts. As one student said, "I like that it keeps my quotes online in one place; I like that I can highlight and capture quotes easily; and I *love* that it creates my works cited."

For adolescents who face an abundance of information each time they search the Web, curating is a crucial skill. Natalie's task asked students to identify a literary work, analyze it and its message, research the historical context and significance of the piece, select additional literature with similar themes, and put the literature in "conversation" with each other, sharing their analysis and the larger conversation with the class via a multimedia presentation. This project, designed as a capstone experience for seniors, required the students to collect, organize, and evaluate multiple sources. Citelighter facilitated this process. The lesson in Figure 6.9 provides an introduction to curating.

Figure 6.8. Lesson plan on making decisions during Web-based reading.

Decisions, Decisions, Decisions

Standards

- CCSS.ELA-Literacy.CCRA.R.7. Integrate and evaluate content presented in diverse media and formats, including visually and quantitatively, as well as in words.
- CCSS.ELA-Literacy.CCRA.R.10. Read and comprehend complex literary and informational texts independently and proficiently.
- CCSS.ELA-Literacy.CCRA.SL.1. Prepare for and participate effectively in a range of conversations and collaborations with diverse partners, building on others' ideas and expressing their own clearly and persuasively.

Rationale

To read and comprehend various kinds of texts (R.10), which include texts of diverse media (R.7), students must make decisions about the texts they choose to read. These decisions involve skills of evaluation that include attention to the reader's immediate purpose, as well as broader intentions. In digital venues, this work is done in conversation with others (SL.1).

Goals

- Students will articulate the choices they make in their out-of-school reading of digital texts.
- Students will identify the larger conversations that surround digital texts.
- Students will reflect on their own reading practices and abilities, specifically identifying their own purposes and intentions.

Formative Assessment

- Students will develop their own "Decision-Making Organizer." See the suggested outline for this assessment below.

Materials

- Decision-Making Organizer (print or digital)
- Computers or e-devices
- Student notebooks/paper/e-devices for reflective writing

Lesson Plan

1. Introduce students to the ideas of short-, mid-, and long-form reading. You might do this by having students sort the types of texts we outline in Chapter 2, categorizing them to develop definitions, or you might provide them with three sample texts and ask them to compare and contrast the nature of each.
2. Once you have a shared definition of short-, mid-, and long-form reading, distribute the Decision-Making Organizer and ask students to be mindful of the reading they do outside of school for the rest of the week.
3. Each day as a "Do Now" or "Closure" activity, ask students to share their reflections with a small group. The group's weeklong purpose will be to develop an answer to the question, "How can we be intentional in deciding what to read digitally?" (NOTE: These discussions are not meant as a full-period lesson. You can focus on other work aside from these check-ins with the groups.)
4. On day 5 ask the groups to finalize their responses to the inquiry question by using evidence from their own practices, collected over the week, to support their claims. Students can display these responses in a variety of ways (e.g., on the class wiki, using poster paper in the classroom). Alternatively, the class can come to consensus on mindful reading practices and add these "Mindful Decisions" to a collective handbook on reading strategies.

continued on next page

Figure 6.8. Continued

Decision-Making Organizer

Weeklong Reflection

Days 1–2: What kinds of digital texts do you encounter and how do you find them?

Today pay attention to what you encounter—on your phone, in your email, or on your computer. Complete the chart.

Short-, Mid-, or Long-form	Name the digital text (e.g., tweet, text message, news article, ebook)	How did you encounter it?

(Add rows as needed)

Day 3: What makes you decide to read a digital text?

Today you should identify 2–4 digital texts that you considered reading.

What was the digital text?	Did you read it?	Why or why not?

(Add rows as needed)

Day 4: What distracts you from reading deeply?

As you read today, be mindful of distractions. When do you find yourself "lost" in your reading and truly engaged? When do you find yourself mindlessly scrolling?

Day 5: What is the value?

Identify one digital text that you encounter today. Ask yourself the following questions and reflect on your decision to read or discard this text:

- Where did this text come from?
- Why did I receive it?
- What value does this article have?
- What are my reading intentions?
- Do I have a specific purpose for reading this text?
- Will it be worth my time to read it?
- What might distract me from reading it deeply?
- Do the distractions matter in this moment?
- How will reading this text allow me to contribute to a larger conversation?

As an extension to this lesson, you can introduce students to the tools that we shared in Chapter 3, such as Clearly or Pocket, to help them think about how to eliminate clutter from their Web-based reading. Additionally, we strongly suggest that you have all students install an extension such as Adblock to eliminate banner ads and in-line ads.

Figure 6.9. Lesson plan on curating digital texts.

Introduction to Curating

Standards

- CCSS.ELA-Literacy.CCRA.R.9. Analyze how two or more texts address similar themes or topics in order to build knowledge or to compare the approaches the authors take.
- CCSS.ELA-Literacy.CCRA.W.1. Write arguments to support claims in an analysis of substantive topics or texts using valid reasoning and relevant and sufficient evidence.
- CCSS.ELA-Literacy.CCRA.W.7. Conduct short as well as more sustained research projects based on focused questions, demonstrating understanding of the subject under investigation.
- CCSS.ELA-Literacy.CCRA.W.8. Gather relevant information from multiple print and digital sources, assess the credibility and accuracy of each source, and integrate the information while avoiding plagiarism.

Rationale

If students are to conduct sustained research projects (W.7) and write arguments for analysis of substantive texts (W.1), they must gather information from multiple digital sources (W.8). They must also analyze how two or more texts work in conversation with each other (R.9) and organize their thinking in relation to those texts so they can revisit them as they develop their arguments. In a world of information overload, students need to develop specific skills of curation in order to meet these goals.

      In this case, we have chosen Citelighter as the curation tool because it allows students to quickly turn their research into a written product with appropriate citations. Evernote and Diigo can serve similar functions but do not export the resources in MLA or APA format or allow for organization of research in the same way that Citelighter does.

Goals

- Students will collect, organize, and evaluate resources based on an inquiry question.
- Students will use a Web-based curating tool to annotate resources in order to fully integrate their ideas into the research project.

Formative Assessment

- Digital "notebook" created in Citelighter or other curation tool

Materials

- Citelighter (or other curating tool such as Evernote or Diigo).
- Computers
- Student notebooks/paper/e-devices for reflective writing

Lesson Plan

1. Model the use of Citelighter, demonstrating how the tool captures information, imports bibliographic information, and allows for commenting.
2. Ask students to reflect in their notebooks on the purposes for each of the following:
   a. Why does capturing the text in the moment matter?
   b. Why does capturing the bibliographic information matter?
   c. Why does being able to comment matter?
3. Facilitate a discussion of these questions, focusing on the idea of "reading now" versus "reading later."
4. Assist students to create Citelighter accounts and to install the Citelighter toolbar on their computers. (At the time of this book's writing, a mobile app for Citelighter was in development but not available. Other

continued on next page

Figure 6.9. Continued

organizational tools discussed in this chapter do have mobile apps but do not necessarily have the same capture features as Citelighter.)

5. As students complete the process of account creation, have them practice capturing, commenting on, and completing bibliographic information by searching for information related to a personal passion (e.g., a sports team, a particular music artist). We recommend starting with nonacademic work to develop familiarity with the tool and to focus students' reflection on why they may want to revisit particular texts at a later time in their out-of-school lives.

6. Ask students to share their discoveries about the tool, as well as their thinking about why curating texts is helpful in both personal and academic life.

7. Assign an academic research task and have students create a "digital notebook" to collect resources and thinking in response to each of the digital texts included.

8. Once students have collected five resources, ask them to analyze two of them in conversation with each other, documenting their thinking in their digital notebook.

In addition to using Citelighter as a tool for curating references for later reading, a number of the other apps mentioned in this book can serve a similar purpose. Pocket, Readability, and Instapaper allow you to save a text for later reading. Diigo and Evernote allow you to save text and annotate it. Keeping the most important items that we've read organized in some coherent manner is crucial as we manage our digital reading lives.

We can identify a variety of strategies you might use with one or more of the tools listed in this lesson. They might include emailing an item to yourself from your mobile device for later reading on the computer, adding a bookmark (Diigo), or downloading for offline reading (Evernote, Pocket, Readability, Instapaper). Also, questions worth asking as you teach students to manage their digital reading lives might include:

- How can students curate and annotate the texts so they are accessible and valuable later on? What tools make the most sense for students as they move across platforms and from school to home?

- Over time we all build up collections of information about a topic. Using tags and other categorization strategies, how can we invite students to reread articles they have saved from a week, a month, or a year ago and compare those to what they read today?

- To support deep, inquiry-based, sustained reading, how can we ask students to begin organizing information now that may connect to other passions and projects that span the rest of the school year, and perhaps beyond?

Because Connected Reading is not a single practice that relies on pre-, during-, and postreading of just one text, we must teach our students how to organize and sustain their reading over time, and these tools can provide such options for them.

Reading Digital Texts

A Connected Reader will engage with digital texts using tried-and-true reading strategies as well as strategies that are unique to reading on a screen. You have probably noticed this yourself, even if you read online materials only every now and again. You and your students must still employ reading strategies. Part of developing these skills involves, as Troy argues in *Crafting Digital Writing* (2013), having students read like digital writers. By evaluating—and taking advantage of—choices that the writer of a digital text makes (e.g., in organization, in use of embedded links, in multimedia features), readers can engage deeply with a text to make meaning.

Although these are important areas for instruction, in talking with teens over the last year we have realized that few organically understand how digital tools can help them to connect to other readers as they engage with a text. For this reason, we focus here on shared reading, and we refer you to our companion wiki to find additional ideas for teaching students to read digital texts mindfully.

Connecting during Reading in Online Spaces

Using many of the tools that we've described in this book so far, we can have students share their reading experience within a given space. Tools like Crocodoc or Diigo allow them to highlight and put notes on a text and then share that reading experience with peers and teachers.

In Chapter 1, we share a screenshot of our shared reading of NCTE's policy research brief *Reading Instruction for* All *Students*. We used Crocodoc to collaboratively annotate the document, which we read asynchronously. We chose Crocodoc because our document was a PDF file, and Crocodoc allows for shared annotations of PDFs. For websites we might choose Diigo, which is described on the "About" page as a "personal knowledge management" multitool.

Diigo has the potential to serve as a curation tool, but what we find most powerful about it is the possibilities for shared annotations. Figure 6.10 is a screenshot of our collaborative thinking about one of Clive Thompson's articles from *Wired* magazine that Troy sent to Kristen early in our drafting of the book. In Diigo, Kristen was able to annotate the article and invite Troy to respond to her initial thoughts. Our conversation evolved from these independent readings, which built on each other because we were able to *see* the other person's thinking about the text.

We discuss the idea of shared annotations in Chapter 5, so here we want to reiterate the power of Connected Reading to contribute to collective thinking and individual reader comprehension. Unlike the annotations we do on a single snapshot, as in Chapter 5, here we can share our thinking across an entire document.

Figure 6.10. Kristen and Troy's annotations of Clive Thompson's online article.

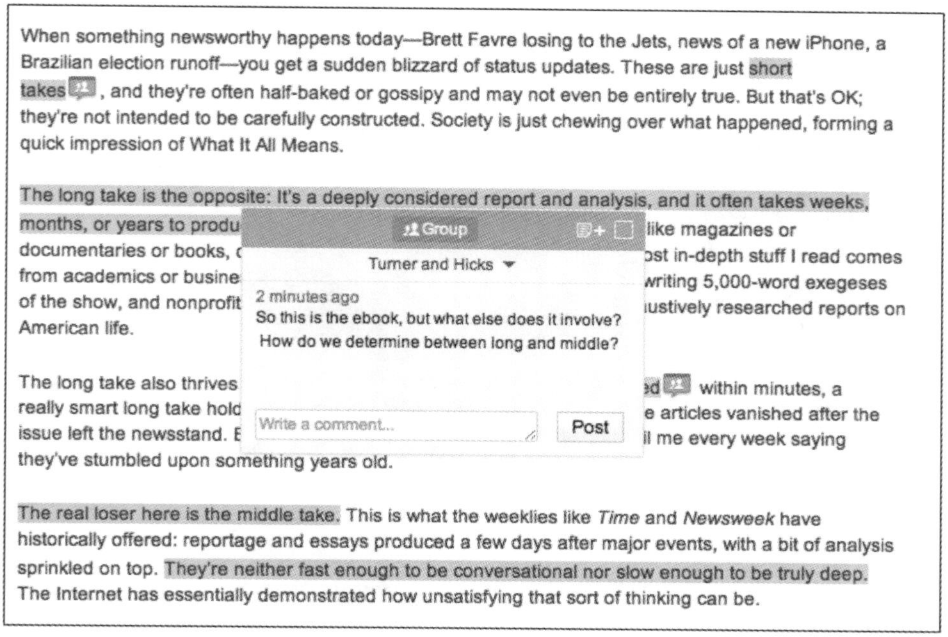

When something newsworthy happens today—Brett Favre losing to the Jets, news of a new iPhone, a Brazilian election runoff—you get a sudden blizzard of status updates. These are just short takes 💬 , and they're often half-baked or gossipy and may not even be entirely true. But that's OK; they're not intended to be carefully constructed. Society is just chewing over what happened, forming a quick impression of What It All Means.

The long take is the opposite: It's a deeply considered report and analysis, and it often takes weeks, months, or years to produ~~~~ like magazines or documentaries or books, ~~~~st in-depth stuff I read comes from academics or busine~~~~writing 5,000-word exegeses of the show, and nonprofit~~~~ustively researched reports on American life.

> 👥 Group   🗨+ ☐
> Turner and Hicks ▾
> 2 minutes ago
> So this is the ebook, but what else does it involve? How do we determine between long and middle?
>
> Write a comment...　　　　　Post

The long take also thrives~~~~ed 💬 within minutes, a really smart long take hold~~~~e articles vanished after the issue left the newsstand. E~~~~il me every week saying they've stumbled upon something years old.

The real loser here is the middle take. This is what the weeklies like *Time* and *Newsweek* have historically offered: reportage and essays produced a few days after major events, with a bit of analysis sprinkled on top. They're neither fast enough to be conversational nor slow enough to be truly deep. The Internet has essentially demonstrated how unsatisfying that sort of thinking can be.

Digging into an Ebook

As we were writing this chapter, President Obama made headlines with his visit to a school that provides iPads to all students. He lauded the effort to engage children in creative thinking by using tools of technology, and he recommitted his ConnectED effort to bringing broadband to all students, regardless of income (Hudson, 2014). With initiatives like this one, more and more schools are bringing tablet technology to the classroom—and with the technology comes the possibility for ebooks to replace print novels.

We know that buying books is not a new idea for English teachers, who evaluate titles, write proposals, and convince school boards to purchase particular texts. But we also know that buying ebooks might be a less familiar practice, and we want to emphasize that there are multiple forms of ebooks you might consider adopting. You may choose to purchase an electronic version of a print novel, but as Itzkovitch (2012) explains, you have other options. He describes three basic formats for ebooks, as shown in Figure 6.11: ebooks, enhanced ebooks, and interactive ebooks.

Figure 6.11. A comparison of ebook functionality.

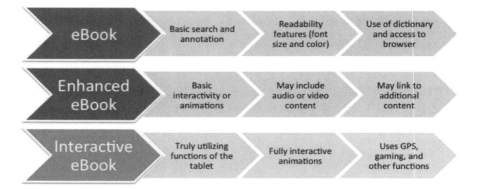

Graphic created by Troy Hicks (@hickstro) based on categories described in:

Itzkovitch, A. (2012, April 12). Interactive eBook Apps: The Reinvention of Reading and
    Interactivity. Retrieved October 3, 2013, from http://uxmag.com/articles/
    interactive-ebook-apps-the-reinvention-of-reading-and-interactivity

The features of ebooks can be summed up as follows:

- Basic search and annotation: Users can search for particular words or phrases using an integrated search function. Additionally, users can "highlight" selected passages that can be collected by the ebook software as a set of notes.

- Readability features: Because of the digital nature of the text itself as an XML or HTML5 format, flowable and adjustable texts have become the norm. No longer do we need to tell students to turn to page X. Instead, we can have them search for words and passages.

- Use of external computing functions: Other useful features of ebooks are the connection to the dictionary and Web-browsing functions. Finding a definition or more information about a word or phrase is literally at one's fingertips simply by pressing and holding a word and launching these additional features.

Enhanced ebook features include all the functions just listed as well as additional materials that enhance the reader's experience and meaning making:

- Basic interactivity such as video and audio clips or animations that begin to work when clicked

- Quizzes or other components that must be completed before moving on in the ebook
- Obvious and inviting links to external content

Finally, interactive ebook features encompass all the functions of the other two types of ebooks, plus applications that use the computing power available on the tablet to integrate maps, games, animation, and other interactive features that would not be possible with a basic ebook reader.

Interactive ebooks can be particularly helpful for struggling readers, as the work of CAST UDL Book Builder (http://bookbuilder.cast.org) has demonstrated. However, it is important for readers to understand the features of these texts to get the most out of their reading. Skipping over links and videos may be problematic when the content in those features is important to making meaning from the text.

Connecting during Reading in an Ebook

Let's imagine that Kristen is preparing to teach a unit on coming of age and the loss of innocence. Her students will be reading *The Adventures of Tom Sawyer* (Twain, 2010) as well as a variety of other texts to support their thinking throughout the unit. However, there are no novels, packets, or sticky notes in the room. Instead, Kristen asks her students to download an app to their iPad: Subtext (www.subtext.com). As students begin this process, Kristen queues up a short video from the Subtext website that demonstrates how students will be able to load a local copy of an ebook so they can read it on- and offline, as well as how they will use Subtext to have conversations via threaded discussion in small reading groups. Kristen also explains that students will download articles and poems that will support their reading over the next few weeks.

As the unit progresses, students annotate the texts in Subtext and hold conversations about the texts within the app. Figure 6.12 provides an example of what this looks like. As the teacher, Kristen can monitor all of her students by looking at the data provided by Subtext, which she has displayed on her own iPad as she walks around the classroom each day, listening to students talk about the annotations their peers made for homework. Groups can continue conversations begun in Subtext the night before, and students can copy and paste quotes directly from the text into Google Docs, gathering evidence for literary essays. Because Subtext shows everyone in the small reading groups what each group member has highlighted, it is easy for students to see quotes of particular importance to their motif for their literary essay. Therefore, before students even begin their group conversations, Kristen asks each of them to identify one helpful comment or question from a classmate in his or her group that he or she read on Subtext the night before.

Figure 6.12. Sample discussion on subtext.

Kristen can also check her students' reading at home each morning before class to determine how many comments and the kinds of responses students have made. She can develop strategic mini-lessons on close reading and gathering evidence for a literary argument based both on what she sees in class and what she is able to view about students' reading outside of class.

The conversations that have been captured on the screen as students annotate the text in Subtext and reflect on their reading in Google Docs will allow Kristen's students to draw on the interpretations of their classmates as they craft their individual essays. Subtext allows a teacher to assess a student's reading as he or she engages with a text in real time, making formative assessment valuable in individualized instruction. As for the readers, Subtext and other tools like it allow them to connect *during* reading in completely new ways.

We offer this particular tool with the recognition that to access some of the features to work for an entire class you would need to purchase a premium subscription. At the time we began writing this book, these features were free to the initial users of Subtext, which has now been purchased by another company. A premium charge now applies. Still, there are other free websites and apps that will allow you and your students to engage in similar kinds of annotation, most notably the suite of tools from Diigo, Ponder, and Curriculet, which include browser extensions and iPad apps. Still, we think that intentional teaching of Connected Reading is made possible by Subtext and is therefore worth sharing. If you are not able to purchase premium versions, many ebook applications allow readers to highlight segments of the text and to see what other readers have highlighted as well. These applications wouldn't be limited to the readers in the classroom but would instead connect students to readers in the world. (We discuss more implications for shifting from print to digital texts, including recommendations for spending, in Chapter 8.)

Sharing Digital Texts

In our survey of adolescents, we saw that a small percentage of them use social networking tools such as Facebook, Twitter, and Google+ to share their thoughts about reading. An even smaller group, approximately 8 percent, engages in social networks dedicated specifically to reading. We hope this is a trend that many of you, as teachers of Connected Reading, are willing to work to reverse.

A number of social networking sites are specifically related to reading. For instance, Goodreads and Shelfari are two popular examples of social networking tools designed for sharing what we are reading. Along with reviews of the book, many users also share relevant quotes. Even if you are not able to have your students sign up for one of these social groups because of age restrictions, you can still use other school-provided social networking sites such as Edmodo or Schoology to create online spaces for your students to share their reading. Getting your students started on any one of the social networking platforms we mention is less of a technical demand than it is a challenge about building community. As with any type of opportunity we use to talk about reading, we want to be sure that students feel both confident and comfortable in sharing their views. As Penny Kittle notes in *Book Love: Developing Depth, Stamina, and Passion in Adolescent Readers* (2013), "A system will not create readers, but the books that keep a reader seeking will" (p. 37). Use social networking to keep your readers seeking, not to institute a new system that demands reading logs of minutes spent and book reviews of a minimum word count.

Rebekah O., the teacher whose testimonial we shared at the beginning of this chapter, hopes to engage her students in broader conversations through their development of personal learning networks. After modeling how she herself uses Twitter to learn, to engage, and to contribute, she offers them the opportunity to use a percentage of their weekly independent reading to curate PLNs, to synthesize their reading using Storify (https://storify.com), and to share that reading with their networks. She walks them through the "why" of this work, constantly modeling her own practice, and she allows them to develop the "how" on their own through experimentation and reflection. They connect all of this work to their Genius Hour (http://geniushour.wikispaces.com/home) projects, which allow them to explore their passions in order to develop academic skills. Rebekah's students are developing practices of Connected Reading that fuel their learning, yet we think you can start smaller—with some of the ideas we've mentioned in this chapter to help students understand the possibilities of response, sharing, and conversation available in reading digital texts.

Evaluating Digital Texts

We mentioned previously that evaluating is a recursive practice of Connected Reading, and we have designed lessons included in this chapter that also build skills of evaluation in deciding, curating, reading, and sharing. Here we consider the judgments students make about a text. Past practice leads many to believe that evaluation equals determining website credibility. In Connected Reading, evaluation is broader.

In the early days of the Internet, determining credibility was a relatively straightforward task. Because domain names were expensive and hosting and maintaining a website were tasks out of reach for most people, it was generally assumed that anyone posting something online either had the authority and ability to do so or they were highly skilled amateurs who might not be experts in any particular content but could make a website look good. Questions on website credibility checklists often included ones related to whether a reader could find reference to a specific author and whether the website itself was aesthetically pleasing. Examples of "fake" or misleading websites were used to show students that they couldn't trust everything on the Internet, most notably a website about Martin Luther King Jr. created by an organization affiliated with the Ku Klux Klan (www.martin lutherking.org).

In subsequent years, a variety of technical innovations such as blogs and wikis have made website publication incredibly easy, as well as aesthetically pleasing, for the average user. Traditional clues to spotting a biased or fake website do not necessarily work as well as they used to because numerous individuals, organizations, and corporations have begun sharing information related to highly controversial topics. For instance, a search on "climate change" can easily lead you to various websites that make claims about humankind's effect (or lack of effect) on the levels of carbon in our atmosphere. In other words, website credibility is no longer about whether the authors have credentials or the site looks nice. It requires a deeper level of reading, in which students are comparing existing knowledge to the information presented online.

These skills involve both judgment of the quality and evaluation of the value of a digital text. Recently, Hagerman and White (2013) proposed their $[(PST)^2 + (iC3)]$ Framework, which includes a variety of strategies that support students as they synthesize online reading. Their "equation" breaks down like this, with two factors for each P, S, and T (hence, the square symbol) and three factors for i and C:

- P: Purpose setting and preexisting knowledge
- S: Search terms and source selection
- T: Type (of text) and trustworthiness of that text
- i: Identify important information
- C: Compare, connect, continually update

These skills are important for Connected Readers, who encounter myriad texts in multiple contexts. Hagerman and White encourage students to evaluate the quality of a text based on ideas related to credibility and importance of information. In addition, we contend that students should also see evaluation as making value judgments about texts: how and why is this text useful for me as a reader and will I share it with my Connected Reading network? Therefore, as we teach our students how to be critical consumers of not only websites but all digital texts, we recommend that they ask questions such as those in the sidebar.

Evaluating Digital Texts

- How did I encounter this digital text (receiving, surfing, stumbling, searching)?

- What is my immediate purpose for reading? What can I gain from engaging with this text?

- What is the purpose of this text? Who is the author? What is the perspective he or she takes?

- What have I read previously and how does it connect with what is presented in this text?

- What are the claims presented? How does the evidence support the claims? Are there links to other sources?

- Should I bring this text into conversations with peers in my networks? What might other readers help me understand if I share this text with them?

Concluding Thoughts on Developing Connected Readers

Our goal in this chapter has been to describe the many types of tools and possibilities available for Connected Reading, especially when you are able to use digital texts. While not all the tools will work for all of your readers, nor do you necessarily want to try to include all of them in your classroom at any one time, we think it important to rethink practice to incorporate intentional instruction surrounding digital texts. It is through this focus that adolescents will develop habits of mindful reading.

We are keenly aware of calls to consider students' passions and out-of-school literacies as we design instruction. We are also aware that co-opting students' personal lives for academic work is not always the best path. What we argue for, then, is honoring students' out-of-school reading and cultivating their abilities to connect with others. For example, one of our survey respondents indicates that she shares her reading with her "fandom." Fan forums are sites for many kinds of texts—including fan fiction—and though we as literature teachers may not find these texts appropriate for literary critique—nor would we necessarily want our students to critique their reading of fan fiction in that vein—we should recognize the passion of the communities.

As adults we can certainly understand what it means to feel passionately about a particular topic, and we must be especially sensitive to this feeling when working with our own students who may be wildly in love with topics we know nothing about. While many scholars and critics would advocate for a more robust use of pop culture in the classroom, and we are not inherently against that position, we want to clarify that reading fan fiction and fan forums can provide our students with opportunities they will not get from other sources we are likely to provide them, and we can honor those reading experiences in the classroom simply by asking students to share what they are reading without assessing what they have read.

Without a doubt, the number of digital texts we encounter will only continue to increase. Oftentimes, when explaining some of the strategies outlined in this chapter to colleagues during workshops, Troy compares the amount of information available online to a fire hydrant, noting that the strategies we use here can help us bring that deluge into something more akin to a drinking fountain. As we move into the final chapters, and we consider the implications of what it means to teach reading for all students, we cannot ignore the prevalence—and usefulness—of digital texts. There are no shortcuts to figuring out how to manage our online reading lives, but these strategies should help.

From Policy Statement to Practice: Instruction and Assessment of Connected Reading

There are lots of pluses to conferencing, but one drawback is that a conferencing cycle can be weeks or even months long, and teachers need assessment data and students need feedback much more frequently. My students' independent reading blogs allowed me to monitor their reading progress, analyze their critical responses to what they read, keep track of the feedback they were providing to one another, and share my own feedback with them. Because they were digital, I could read blogs anywhere, including on my iPhone. Students received far more feedback from their peers through the blog than they did from me. More important, students might receive one comment from me, but they could receive comments from twenty or more of their peers in a single day. I used the blogs to monitor progress, plan instruction, and determine individual conferencing priorities, while students used blogs to share ideas, discuss texts, experiment with different ways to express themselves using digital tools, and engage with others in intellectual text-based arguments. The blog, whose intent was originally about formative assessment of reading skills, became a forum for students to practice their writing skills as well. I've always thought that the best assessments are instructional, and that's what the blog became: a formative assessment that was also in itself an instructional experience for students. (Rebekah S., grade 12 teacher)

Remember that all links and handouts are located on the companion wiki. Scan this QR code or go to http:// connectedreading .wikispaces.com to access Chapter 7 materials.

Rebekah used reading logs to monitor her students' independent reading progress nearly every year she taught. Though she worked with seniors, many of them required support in their reading. She used the logs to identify areas in which her students needed instruction, and she adjusted her daily lessons accordingly. However, she knew there was a lag between the students' work, her assessment, and her responsive instruction. She also knew that because the students wrote their logs only for her, they saw them simply as another task to complete, and many students did not submit them.

When Rebekah turned reading logs digital, she did more than change the audience for students' writing about their reading; she also shifted the nature of assessment and feedback. Assessment became instantaneous, and Rebekah, able to check her students' progress from her smartphone while on the go or from her classroom computer, could alter her instruction immediately in response to her students' work. Even more important, however, she noticed the teens giving one another feedback on the blogs. They were connected as readers, pushing one another's thinking and supporting comprehension across the class.

The shift in Rebekah's classroom from print-based reading logs to reading response blogs represents a move toward what we identify as "Connected Reading instruction" (CRI). CRI focuses on the practices of Connected Reading outlined in Chapter 2 and summarized on our Connected Reading model (see Figure 2.1 on p. 21). Connected Reading is a variety of interconnected practices that honors individual readers. At the center of the model is the reader him- or herself; the reader's own attributes and abilities, the reading context, and textual features all influence comprehension. The reader's practices include encountering, engaging, and evaluating texts, both print and digital. This process happens in a social context, influenced by the teacher, peers, and a broader, networked community of readers and writers. Finally, this model builds on comprehension strategy instruction, sociocultural approaches to literacy, new literacies, textual and hypertextual features, and connected learning; each of these perspectives provides insight into how readers make meaning with a variety of texts, and combined they help us see that contemporary reading practices are highly mediated social experiences. In sum, Connected Reading is a model that honors individual readers within a reading community that spans beyond the classroom, acknowledges a variety of textual forms, and recognizes the process of meaning making that can occur when using digital devices and networks in mindful ways. It presents us with a new set of intellectual opportunities as readers, and we encourage you to develop your own Connected Reading practices as you teach them to students. We believe that *being* a Connected Reader, and reflecting on your practices as such, is the first step toward CRI.

Moreover, CRI allows teachers to use digital tools to maximize opportunities for them to see students' thinking and respond to it, the double helix of formative assessment. When teachers can immediately see their students' thinking, they can tailor their instruction to meet the needs of each student, providing digital feedback, in-class conferences, whole-class mini-lessons, or other forms of instruction. In this way, CRI supports reading for *all* students through effective use of technology. We also recommend turning to the research that has already been done in the field of reading instruction as you consider how to best teach Connected Reading. The NCTE policy research brief *Reading Instruction for* All *Students* synthesizes this research into eight implications for instructional policy. We examine each in turn, noting the role that a Connected Reading perspective can bring to these implications.

Implications for Connected Reading Instruction (CRI)

Recognize the role that motivation plays in students' reading by modeling for students with complex texts that do and do not interest them.
The roles of motivation and interest have become only more prominent in discussions of adolescent literacy in the decade since Smith and Wilhelm's (2002) publication of *"Reading don't fix no Chevys."* With the proliferation of texts for teens to read, as well as devices for them to read with, students have access to a variety of stories, articles, books, and other forms of reading material. While balancing our need to meet curricular standards, we must also encourage students to use the Web and mobile apps to find relevant, timely materials that support their own personal interests and academic pursuits. In helping students to discover texts related to the content they are studying—and inviting them to share their interpretations of those texts across social networks and in wider conversations—we have the potential to help provide students with opportunities for sustained, long-form reading as well as micro-bursts of short- and mid-form reading that can fuel their learning.

Rebekah O. (Chapter 6), for instance, shows us how this connection of personal and academic reading can live together in the classroom through her personal learning network (PLN) assignment, in which she asks students to develop networks that will contribute to their Genius Projects. Deliberately sharing her own PLN and modeling her reading practices help her students to see the habits of a Connected Reader and to consider how seemingly meaningless tweets or status updates may have underlying complexities that can lead to deep reading and deep thinking.

Engage students in performative reading responses such as gesture, mime, vocal intonation, characterization, and dramatization to enable active construction of meaning, and construct a collaborative environment that builds on the strengths of individual students.
In an era when STEM dominates many discussions about education, we must reiterate the value of performance and artistic creativity. Certainly,

performance can happen in the classroom, but it can also happen beyond the walls of the classroom. In earlier chapters, we describe a variety of tools and techniques for annotating, responding to, and extending our comprehension through Connected Reading practices. Rather than being a mundane task, reporting on our reading can become performative opportunities.

For example, Lauren (Chapter 5) asked her students to create PSAs in response to their reading of *Fist, Knife, Stick, Gun* (Canada, 2010), in essence inviting them to vocalize and dramatize their reading. By sharing their videos publicly, they found value in the assignment, and even her most reluctant readers and writers completed the task. The collaboration inherent in Lauren's activity allows individual students to demonstrate strengths (e.g., video editing, scripting), and she takes advantage of digital tools to archive student performance, which can be viewed and analyzed time and again, living beyond a one-shot presentation in the classroom.

Have students read multiple texts focused on the same topic to improve comprehension through text-to-text connections.

Rethinking the cognitive task and the tools students can use to complete a reading assignment are both important considerations as we ask students to read multiple texts that are focused on the same topic. It is the conversation that matters—the larger conversation that situates the text and the immediate conversation that a teen reader might have with the text or with other readers of the text. Within our approach to Connected Reading, digital tools can facilitate, make transparent, and archive the conversations surrounding students' reading practices in authentic and productive ways.

Natalie's seniors (Chapter 6) read many kinds of texts as they complete their senior research projects, and their use of Citelighter helps them to curate these texts and make text-to-text connections, both in their papers and in their formal presentations to the class. Though traditional research papers also ask students to read multiple texts, we believe that Natalie's assignment is different in that it asks students to put texts in conversation with each other rather than simply summarize or summarize information from these texts. Additionally, Natalie believes it important that students find texts that are interesting to them, and she encourages the incorporation of music, nonfiction, and fiction into their inquiries.

Foster students' engagement with complex texts by teaching students how different textual purposes, genres, and modes require different strategies for reading.

As we articulated in our model of Connected Reading, comprehension strategy instruction has provided adolescent readers with the base they need to further explore complex texts. We know this approach works for print-based texts, and we see great promise in transferring comprehension strategy instruction to digital texts for classroom instruction. We have provided examples of how teachers have been turning strategy instruction digital, and we shared particular strategies that adolescent readers have identified from their own reading. Digital tools allow us to truly "make our thinking visible," and sharing that thinking with other readers is one way that we can invite our students to become more effective with their own reading.

While accessing texts through various technologies is an important first step, we must also be conscious of our efforts to help students engage with those texts using digital tools. At a very basic level, this involves simple annotations and gathering quotations. At a more complex, sophisticated level, we can invite students to engage in conversations and produce new media based on their understandings of what they have read. Again, using technology in a manner that moves students into the roles of both producer and consumer of text means they will be evaluating, synthesizing, and sharing rather than just comprehending.

Dawn (Chapter 5), for instance, asks her students to identify motifs across an entire book, *To Kill a Mockingbird*, by taking pictures of the text and annotating them for close reading. In doing so, she describes the ways in which students' collaboration led to deeper understandings of this complex text, ultimately leading to their group presentations on motifs. While she could have accomplished some of the same goals through the use of sticky notes and in-class discussions, she found that students' opportunities to engage with the text, both inside and outside of school, yielded positive results.

Encourage students to choose texts, including nonfiction, for themselves, in addition to assigned ones, to help them see themselves as capable readers who can independently use reading skills they learn in class.

Although quantitative and qualitative measures of text complexity are important—and we certainly want students to engage in print-based reading—we must also invite students to pursue a variety of diverse texts that include linear texts in a digital format (basic ebooks), hypertexts (such as webpages and interactive ebooks), and texts that are highly dependent on multimedia and interactivity (such as a multimedia-based ebook or the websites for *Inanimate Alice* or *Snowfall*). Ideally, selections of texts could be both fiction and nonfiction, encouraging students to explore various genres as they also engage in new media comprehension.

Helping students to become active, independent readers certainly involves choosing the right book for the right reader, and we applaud our colleagues who work to inspire a love of reading in their students. We want to move their ideas one step further; teaching students how to access and share these types of diverse texts through social networks, online libraries, RSS feeds, and other digital spaces should become a crucial part of reading instruction. We must also teach the types of decision-making skills that will allow our students to read on the Web and with various ebook formats too, and this is a pressing need for classroom instruction and modeling.

One of the first steps in this process involves asking students to reflect on the kinds of texts they already read. Our "Decisions, Decisions, Decisions" lesson (Chapter 6) helps adolescents to name their short-, mid-, and long-form reading habits and find value in each type of text. This allows them to see their reading practices as important in a way they may not have recognized before, and yet they can still set goals to improve as readers.

Demonstrate, especially at the secondary level, how digital and visual texts, including multimodal and multigenre texts, require different approaches to reading.

While the focus of this is, intentionally, on helping students make meaning primarily from alphabetic text, both in print and on screen, both of us are quick to note that reading—in the broadest sense of interpretation, inference, and comprehension—requires students to analyze and respond to various other forms of media as well, including images and video. In our efforts to teach Connected Reading, we will encounter texts that draw on a variety of other interpretive skills and demand a full range of expression for response, as we have shown with many of the lesson ideas and examples in this book. Books are, quite simply, no longer just printed words on pages, as even many books, like this one, have a companion website or other online supplements. For instance, Troy used QR codes in his most recent book to connect readers with Web-based resources, and authors now often address readers directly and encourage them to visit a website or watch a video before continuing to read. And, of course, ebooks that allow more and more interactivity are quickly becoming popular.

As we demonstrated with our brief example of Subtext (Chapter 6), the point here is not that a print-based text has been made digital, or simply more convenient. Though that is a nice feature, what is more important is that the text will now allow for—and, in fact, require—students to draw on new strategies for comprehension and interaction with both the text itself and other readers. Being digital is not, in this case, a novelty. Digital texts provide readers with new and different options, and we must teach our students how to take advantage of those opportunities.

Connect students' reading of complex texts with their writing about reading and with writing that uses complex texts as models so they will recognize and be able to negotiate many different types of complex texts.

Composition research, especially in the past twenty years, demonstrates that students are much more successful at writing in a variety of genres, especially academic genres, when provided with models and encouraged to use those models in generative, rather than formulaic, ways. For instance, reading a number of op-eds from major news sources as well as blog posts from independent writers and then discussing the rhetorical moves that each writer makes can lead to practice of those moves, followed by integration of such moves into a writer's own repertoire.

We want our students as Connected Readers to be mindful of these moves in all texts across genres, especially those that offer hypertextual, interactive features. Understanding how and why unique features such as links, embedded media, and aesthetics can contribute to a reader's ability to make meaning remains an important task for digital writers and should be taught explicitly. Connected Readers must learn to, as Troy has argued in various publications, "read like digital writers" in order to take full advantage of the text features available for assisting in comprehension.

Develop students' ability to engage in meaningful discussion of the complex texts they read through whole-class, small-group, and partner conversations so they can learn to negotiate and comprehend complex texts independently.

Connected Reading is in many ways like reading in a traditional sense. We know that sharing our reading with others has always been an important component of comprehension. Yet, like Knobel and Lankshear (2006), who remind us that a change in technologies can provide us new opportunities for literacies if we also change our approach, we want to stress that Connected Reading gives our students the opportunity to engage in conversations with their peers (and others) quickly, seamlessly, and transparently. This is more than a change in technology. It is a change in behavior and, to use Knobel and Lankshear's term, *mindset*. Reading in our contemporary world requires us to approach both print and digital texts with mindfulness and intention.

As demonstrated throughout this book, especially in Chapters 5 and 6 with the examples of annotating pictures from print texts, as well as the use of Subtext and Diigo, students must have ample opportunity to make their own thinking visible and to share that thinking with their peers. The simple categories of pre-, during-, and postreading no longer apply in a model of Connected Reading. Therefore, we need to make an expectation of transparency and participation the new norm when it comes to reading instruction, and these habits will lead to meaningful discussions and comprehension of complex texts.

Implications for Assessment

In a recent policy brief, the Assessment Task Force of NCTE (2013) defines formative assessment as

> the lived, daily embodiment of a teacher's desire to refine practice based on a keener understanding of current levels of student performance, undergirded by the teacher's knowledge of possible paths of student development within the discipline and of pedagogies that support such development. At its essence, true formative assessment is assessment that is informing—to teachers, students, and families. (p. 2)

Formative assessment allows teachers to make immediate and ongoing decisions about instruction, and it allows students to be involved in that process. Fisher and Frey (2007) argue that "formative assessments are ongoing assessments, reviews, and observations in a classroom. Teachers use formative assessment to improve instructional methods and provide student feedback throughout the teaching and learning process" (p. 4). Additionally, Benjamin (2013) has devoted an entire book to the processes of formative assessment in ELA classrooms. She provides examples of formative assessments in reading that range from read-alouds to summarizing to creating questions about the reading. Formative assessment should be the most powerful type of assessment in schools.

Reading Instruction for All *Students* provides a variety of examples of high-quality formative assessment, such as having students (1) acknowledge background experiences, (2) think aloud while reading complex texts, (3) identify personal interests, and (4) differentiate between various kinds of texts and the effect they have on reading comprehension. All of these strategies promote self-monitoring for students and individualized instruction from teachers.

As Rebekah S.'s reflection at the beginning of this chapter indicates, digital tools can assist in this kind of instantaneous feedback for students and teachers. Rebekah is able to see her students' reading progress without carrying around a stack of student notebooks filled with reading logs. She can check in anytime, anyplace, and because of this access, she can focus on the needs of individual students in an immediate way. Dawn and Jen (Chapter 5) were likewise able to see the close reading practices of their students. Through digital annotations and Google presentations in Dawn's class, individuals, peer groups, and the teacher received real-time information about comprehension. Likewise, in Jen's lessons, screen capture tools enabled think-alouds to become permanent documentations that linked verbal thoughts to specific areas of a text. With these verbal thoughts recorded on screen, Jen can (re)visit them to assess students' progress.

In whatever manner this process of assessment happens—working with technology tools; in our individual, face-to-face conversations with students; as well as through in-class discussions via literature circles and Socratic seminars—NCTE (2013) advocates that formative assessments should come from observations, conversations, student self-evaluations, and authentic artifacts of learning. The focus on individual learners, as well as their processes of learning, must be at the center of our assessment practices. You understand how difficult this process can be based on work with your own students. Still, these are practices worth maintaining and expanding with the use of digital tools.

Digital tools, we argue, can help make this learning visible and provide instantaneous feedback that can inform instruction. More important, these tools can also be employed as students develop projects, essays, performances, and other artifacts for summative assessment. NCTE defines *summative assessment* as "after-the-fact assessment in which we look back at what students have learned, such as end-of-course or end-of-year examinations" (NCTE and IRA, 2009). Beyond exams, there are certainly other ways of summatively assessing students' work, including cumulative portfolios, performance-based projects, and presentations prepared for audiences outside the classroom. Connected Reading can play a role in the ways that students prepare for these types of summative assessment activities.

Though we see many opportunities for formative and summative assessment practices that can help students grow as Connected Readers, when we begin to look at the current efforts for assessing reading that have come to pass under the CCSS, we are quite concerned about the nature of standardized assessments.

Perhaps the most widely discussed form of reading assessment today focuses on the Lexile levels of student readers, and as we said in Chapter 1, we (as well as many other experts in reading comprehension) are baffled by the prominence of Lexile measures in matching readers with texts. As our model of Connected Reading articulates, comprehension comprises many factors; textual features, which include but are not limited to text complexity, are only part of the equation. This notion is particularly true when we examine hyperlinked or multimedia texts. How do these text features contribute to a text's complexity? What happens when a reader moves outside of one text to another (of a different complexity) through a hyperlink? How does a reader make meaning across these various forms of texts? These are all questions of reading assessment that cannot be answered by Lexile measures alone.

We have also heard the comment within discussions of standardized reading assessment that new tests, which will be taken on a computer, are inherently measuring skills of digital reading. We disagree strongly with this claim. Most, if not all, of the large-scale, technology-driven reading assessment tools (e.g., Accelerated Reader, Read 180), as well as the sample items released by PARCC and SBAC, do not measure practices of Connected Reading. In fact, they do not measure much more than skills of basic comprehension. In a comparison of various assessments—including the Diagnostic Assessment of Reading (DAR), the Iowa Test of Basic Skills, and the Scholastic Reading Inventory (SRI)—Morsy, Kieffer, and Snow (2010) found that most standardized assessments were focused on comprehension strategies for identifying main idea and making inferences but not on critical analysis or synthesis (p. 9). The new PARCC and SBAC sample items fall in the same trap, and most of the questions we have seen do not recognize the complexity of reading digital texts. If assessments do not address how students encounter, engage with, and evaluate texts in a digital world, they do not measure skills of Connected Reading, regardless of whether they are given on a computer.

Though the reading assessments just mentioned do not align with practices of Connected Reading, the Online Reading Comprehension Assessments (ORCA) project (Coiro & Kennedy, 2011) is moving in the right direction. As the designers of the project describe it, ORCA will capture "real-time" online reading products and processes while individuals read for information on the Internet. The underlying design of any ORCA is informed by a new literacies perspective of online reading comprehension that frames reading comprehension as a web-based problem-solving inquiry process involving skills and strategies for locating, critically evaluating, synthesizing, and communicating information on the Internet (p. 5)

The project aims to create "an authentic, problem-based scenario situated in a digital environment that engages seventh grade students in a series of online disciplinary information requests" (p. 13). By focusing on skills—*locate*, *evaluate*, *synthesize*, and *communicate* (LESC)—ORCA asks students to work in hyperlinked environments and to demonstrate the capacities of digital reading. These skills are critical and, indeed, embedded in our model of Connected Reading, which draws on the work of Leu and Coiro, the leaders of the ORCA project.

However, as we consider what standardized assessment of Connected Reading will include, our surveys and interviews with adolescent readers strongly suggest that teen readers—or adults, for that matter—do not always open up a Web browser with the intention of locating information, as our categories of receiving and stumbling show. Although the type of task embedded in the ORCA assessment makes sense, we also know that locating and evaluating information does not happen in a vacuum. ORCA, according to the description provided in their report, will be limiting assessment to issues of searching; there will be no social interactions in the simulated activity, nor will it account for other practices highlighted in our model. Our understanding of Connected Reading suggests that this simply is not how the Web, or anyone searching the Web, works.

In short, as with any standardized assessment, we run into the situation in which a particular task, labeled as authentic, must actually be quite tightly controlled for the assessment to work. We have known for a long time that reading assessments by means of standardized test are not always the best measures of what readers actually know and can do. We fear the same will happen with standardized tests related to online reading comprehension. We do not view these types of wide-scale assessments in the same way we see formative assessment. Formative assessment is ongoing, and it is a stance that teachers take in the classroom to guide students as they learn. Therefore, it is absolutely essential that we, as teachers working with readers every day, use formative assessment to guide our instruction and also inform researchers and policymakers about the ways that students are really reading. Digital tools can help achieve these goals.

Moving toward Connected Reading Instruction

Connected Reading instruction capitalizes on the features of digital tools to develop the skills of Connected Readers by providing both the means for reading connections and the possibility for formative assessment. We have shared many ideas throughout the book to achieve the goals of CRI, and Figure 7.1 summarizes just a few instruction and assessment opportunities when teaching Connected Reading.

Figure 7.1. Connected Reading instruction and assessment.

Connected Reading Instruction	
Understanding personal reading practices in print and digital contexts • Survey reading habits • Set goals • Interview fellow students	Reflecting on specific reading activities • Think aloud (screencasts for digital texts, video recording for print texts) • Annotate digitally (screenshots for digital texts, pictures of print texts)
Developing personalized reading experiences • Set up RSS feeds • Create PLNs • Storify reading • Participate in social networks	Reading strategically • Search engine analysis • Reflect on path for reading • Compare/contrast texts
Engaging in collaborative close reading • Use tools for research and annotation • Collaboratively annotate • Respond to one another's annotations	Responding to reading • Create digital literature circles • Compose digital book trailers/multimedia response • Submit online book reviews

Assessment Opportunities

- Digital reading journals
- Goal setting related to authors, sources, genres, and a mix of short-, mid-, and long-form reading (goals should depend on more than just total minutes or number of texts read)
- Digital annotations or screencasts to see evidence of close and critical reading
- Think-aloud screen captures to describe a typical Web-browsing session, showing how the student chooses a particular reading path
- Screen captures or screencasts that create periodic snapshots of RSS reading
- Summaries of important articles from RSS reading, using literary and disciplinary vocabulary to describe the posts
- Reflections that document one's experience with reading in a particular (digital) genre over time, comparing and contrasting author's point of view and rhetorical techniques
- Analysis of similarities and differences of short-, mid-, and long-form articles on a news-related topic as it develops (for instance, as a breaking news story moves from tweets, to initial releases, to analysis in the weeks after)
- Multimodal performative responses that demonstrate substantive knowledge of a specific text

These recommendations for Connected Reading instruction and assessment suggest that teachers balance whole-class with individualized reading instruction, inviting students to make choices about what they read while also sharing their comprehension and meaning making. They also encourage the use of digital tools to purposefully conduct formative assessments that will allow you to see the reading processes and practices of your students. We would not specifically prescribe any single combination of practices and tools for you and your students, and we look forward to ongoing conversations about the approaches you find valuable.

Inquiry and Advocacy

Digital reading makes reading very accessible for people . . . and our generation
has pretty much grown up with a computer in hand, so maybe it will bring books
into the modern era. . . . It's not so much about the books as it is about the stories,
and I think books are a great platform to share stories. So I'm pro-reading [books],
but I'm just saying that not everyone likes it, and so you need to make it fun and
relevant for kids. (Sienna, grade 9)

For as long as the two of us have been in education, there have been numerous,
almost countless, calls to action for adolescent literacy. In the early 2000s and
right up to today, a number of teacher-researchers, most notably Cris Tovani,
Penny Kittle, Kelly Gallagher, and Donalyn Miller, as well as university-based
researchers such as Michael Smith and Jeffrey Wilhelm, have worked to remind
us that reading is not, and should not be, a chore. Recent titles of their books
remind us of this simple truth:

Remember that all links and handouts are located on the companion wiki. Scan this QR code or go to http://connectedreading .wikispaces.com to access Chapter 8 materials.

- *Readicide: How Schools Are Killing Reading and What You Can Do about It* (Gallagher, 2009)
- *Book Love: Developing Depth, Stamina, and Passion in Adolescent Readers* (Kittle, 2013)
- *The Book Whisperer: Awakening the Inner Reader in Every Child* (Miller, 2009)
- *So What Do They Really Know? Assessment That Informs Teaching and Learning* (Tovani, 2011)
- *Reading Unbound: Why Kids Need to Read What They Want—And Why We Should Let Them* (Wilhelm & Smith, 2014)

Of course, we could add to this list many others who write about adolescent literacy. All of them share a mission: to help teens love reading. To that end, we agree with our colleagues who are passionate advocates for helping adolescents love books. Books are clearly an important component of a person's reading life, and we in no way want to detract from the power of story, the pull of a persuasive argument, or the kinds of in-depth information that can be shared in books. Thus, Sienna's point that reading is "not so much about the books as it is about the stories" and that we need to make reading "fun and relevant" hits on a variety of issues we've argued for here.

Books are undoubtedly important, but we also want to encourage all teachers, especially teachers of English, to consider the variety of texts that students can find—as well as the engaging, immersive experiences they can have—with Connected Reading. We have shared many caveats throughout the book related to the ways in which students may skim, or randomly click on links, or be distracted by other features on their laptops, tablets, and smartphones. The opportunity for distraction, as many critics would remind us, can create teens who aren't really readers at all, who instead skim and scan text while watching videos and playing games. We understand the fear that new technologies might contribute to a culture of nonreaders, or less-than-competent readers, yet the teens in our study showcase the opposite—they represent a range of readers who engage with a variety of texts.

From their own self-described reading practices, we have painted a compelling picture of why and how digital texts matter to teens, as well as ways to teach our students mindful, strategic approaches to these texts. Our survey data have duplicated what Pew Internet has been telling us for years: teens are online, and more of them have access now than ever. Because of device ownership, access to texts is changing as ebooks become more popular and individuals consume more news on the go. Just because texts have become increasingly digital does not mean that teens are less likely to engage with them. A love of reading today requires more than just a connection to books; it requires us to teach Connected Reading.

This approach has implications for teaching and learning. *Reading Instruction for All Students* highlights a few:

> Reading research shows that educational policy needs to include professional development opportunities that enable teachers to match instructional approaches to diverse student needs. In order to support teachers' ability to draw on a complex set of instructional approaches in service of diverse learner reading outcomes, teachers need frequent and sustained opportunities to learn with one another about the range of instructional supports, interventions, and formative assessments as they emerge from the latest reading research and practice. (p. xiii–xiv)

A shift in thinking about the nature of reading requires that educators talk with one another about the practices of real-world readers, not just the limited skills that are tested or the standards that can be linked to instruction. This work requires a stance of inquiry, which frames the recommendations we make in this chapter.

Professional Development as Inquiry

In their book *Inquiry as Stance: Practitioner Research for the Next Generation*, Cochran-Smith and Lytle (2009) claim,

> Inquiry as stance is neither a top-down nor a bottom-up theory of action, but an organic and democratic one that positions practitioners' knowledge, practitioners, and their interactions with students and other stakeholders at the center of educational transformation. (pp. 123–24)

Inquiry as stance places teachers as agents in their own development, and we believe this view mirrors the "organic and democratic" nature of Connected Reading in which readers engage with texts suggested by others, participate in conversations about those texts, and contribute to questions—and answers—through a network. Since Connected Reading is in itself a stance of inquiry, so too must be professional development related to CRI.

NCTE, as outlined in their "Principles of Professional Development" position statement, believes that "professional development relies on a rich mix of resources, including a theoretical and philosophical base; a research base; and illustrations of good practices" (2006). We have argued elsewhere that changing what we do in literacy instruction is vital to the development of our students (Hicks & Turner, 2013), and we see this change not merely as a simple insertion of technology into the classroom. Instead, it requires substantive change. In summary, we argued that:

> English teachers are overwhelmed by initiatives, standards, and high-stakes assessments. However, the concerns we outline in this article cannot be pushed aside. Over

the years, teachers of English have rallied against censorship, fought for the inclusion of diverse voices in the canon of literature, and recognized the power of out-of-school literacies. Now English teachers must embrace a new role: We must advocate for digital literacy, not just technology, in a way that reconceptualizes our discipline. We must dump the dittos, throw out the workbooks, and remix our teaching for a digital age. (p. 61)

As we shift our thinking about what it means to teach Connected Reading, we must adopt a new mindset toward technology use. We both hear arguments (usually from parents who think that technology distracts from learning more than it assists) that PowerPoints do not help learning and that districts are spending too much money on technology when they should be focusing on other issues. We hear the validity in these arguments when technology is simply used as a substitute for what we have always done in the past. In this case, we would agree with critics who argue that we do not need to purchase $1,000 pencils.

However, smartphones, tablets, laptops, and other digital devices are much, much more than $1,000 pencils.

To understand this stance, of course, requires a change in mindset toward teaching and learning with digital devices. Puentedura (2010, 2014) has helped us think about technology and its role in teaching and learning. He articulates a framework of substitution, augmentation, modification, and redefinition—SAMR—that is useful in reflecting on what we teach as well as why we do so (see Figure 8.1). SAMR helps us think about the need to redefine both the nature of the *content* we want students to learn as well as the *skills* we teach them. As indicated in the graphic, the use of technology at the "substitution" level involves no substantial change in thinking about how the tool itself works. In this case, we are indeed providing children with $1,000 pencils because there has been no change in teaching practice. Imagine, for instance, that instead of having students pick up a paper copy of *Great Expectations*, we simply asked them to download a copy from Project Gutenberg as a PDF. They would save this PDF on their own smartphone or tablet for convenient reading, but it would not involve a substantive change in how we plan to teach with the text because we are making no efforts to foster collaborative reading or response.

Moving up to the next level, "augmentation," we could ask students to download *Great Expectations* through the Kindle app, thus allowing them to create their own annotations in the ebook, and then to copy and paste those annotations into their own reading log in Google Docs. This document could then be shared with the teacher or other members of their reading group as a way to invite comments and response. In either case, however, individual readers are still working alone most of the time, on their own devices, to make meaning. While they may

Figure 8.1. Puentedura's SAMR model of technology integration (used with permission).

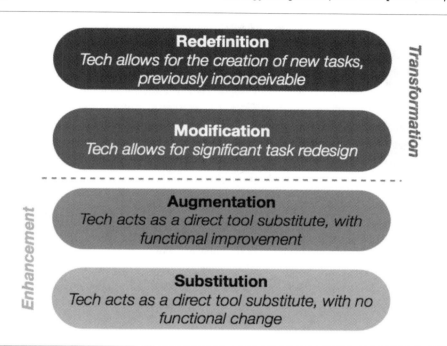

cooperate with one another in a Google Doc, they are not really collaborating to the full extent the technology would allow.

Using the iPad in this manner to simply "enhance" the reading experience is not enough. For us, Connected Reading is more than transferring print texts to screen and transferring traditional reading practices from paper to pixels. Connected Reading involves new kinds of texts and new kinds of practices, and we therefore need to redefine how we teach reading to help students be successful consumers of information (and pleasure reading) in a digital age. Moving "up" on the SAMR scale, then, is a critical component in the process of CRI.

Imagine a task that might involve "modification." The teacher could use Subtext as a tool to share the digital version of *Great Expectations* with the entire class. She could also create assignments that allowed students to read the text together in small groups, responding to questions and offering feedback to one another about their interpretations. This task would involve real-time collaboration and meaning making. To move it up another level, "redefinition" of the reading task might ask students not only to engage in discussions via Subtext but also to then articulate points of confusion in the text. Students could perhaps take a screenshot of a difficult passage for annotation (as we described in Chapter 5) and then use a screen recording tool such as Educreations or Explain Everything to record a think-aloud about the text, sharing it with their group.

In this manner, students are interacting with the digital version of the text in ways that a print book simply cannot emulate. On the SAMR model, both of these types of activities involve "transformation," asking students to engage in activities and create products about *Great Expectations* that could never have been accomplished without the technology. Indeed, if we stay at the "substitution" or "augmentation" level, then critics who believe that technology is simply a distraction from real work may have a point. Transformation, on the other hand, engages students in activities that involve high levels of creative and critical thinking.

Thus, SAMR is a useful framework for thinking about professional development, both at the individual and the collective levels, and we encourage you to keep redefinition in mind as you read our recommendations for professional development, which include creating a personal learning network (PLN) and connecting with other educators through professional organizations. Through a PLN, you can embody a stance of inquiry about your own practices of Connected Reading as well as those of your students.

Creating a Personal Learning Network

At one level, all professional development is a personal choice. Whether we choose to engage with an after-school workshop, a Web seminar, a conference session, or any other professional development (PD) opportunity is up to individual teachers. Though states and districts can mandate requirements, the heart of PD depends on an individual's active participation. We must engage in our own learning. While this statement seems obvious, it has become even more important in our modern era when budget cuts and increasing demands for recertification confront us.

In other words, we must pay attention to our own individual growth. Richardson (2010), who argues for the redefinition of classrooms through the use of technologies such as blogs, wikis, and podcasts, reveals an important aspect of professional development: "While there is no doubt my classes were in many ways profoundly changed by blogs, wikis, and the like, the bigger truth is that the transformation in my own personal learning practice is what informed my work with students" (p. 8). Richardson suggests that teachers must be *users* before they ask their students to engage with technologies so that they understand "how these technologies could facilitate global connections and conversations" (p. 8). Similarly, the National Writing Project (n.d.) advocates that teachers of writing must be writers themselves in order to embrace the struggles and to experience the joys of writing and of sharing their work within a community. Likewise, we advocate that teachers develop their practices of Connected Reading, developing their PLN to include a larger community of readers who engage in global conversations.

Richardson and Mancabelli (2011) state that personal learning networks alter our "fundamental understandings of how learning networks work" (p. 34) and document a number of "guideposts" for this type of learning, including (1) uncovering passion to learn, (2) sharing, (3) reflecting, and (4) growing face-to-face networks (p. 35). Because PLNs are inherently digital, growing a PLN requires many technical skills—learning how to use Twitter, managing RSS feeds, following educational thought leaders—but it also requires a new mindset toward learning.

All of the teachers in our study engaged as Connected Readers outside of the classroom through their PLNs, and they saw value in bringing those practices to their students. Some of the teachers, such as Dawn and Jeremy, have worked at digital literacy for many years, developing connections over time, trying new technologies, and experimenting with new forms of digital texts. Others, like Rebekah O., Lauren, and Rebekah S., jumped in recently, feet first while sometimes holding their breath, and have seen a dramatic transformation in both their personal lives and their teaching practices in a very short time. Clearly, there is no one path for us all to follow in this world of personalized professional learning. Figure 8.2 provides a few ideas for developing your own practices of Connected Reading and extending your PLN, although there are countless others you can pursue. Also, these are just thumbnail sketches to get started; links to other online material that will help with step-by-step learning can be found on our wiki: https://connected reading.wikispaces.com.

Dip your toes in the stream of edublogging, tweeting, and social networking. Create your PLN. Engage in Connected Reading. By doing so, you will adopt a stance of inquiry that will fuel your classroom practice.

We are sure you will not sink and instead will soon choose to swim with thousands of colleagues from around the country and around the world.

Rethinking Classroom Practice

Connected Reading instruction builds on what research has shown to be effective reading pedagogy, and a first step in shifting from the development of your own Connected Reading practices to those of your students might be to consider how to evolve the practices that we suspect you already have in place.

Zemelman, Daniels, and Hyde (2012) summarize a number of research-based recommendations for teaching reading. We have condensed and highlighted some

Figure 8.2. Using Connected Reading to develop a personal learning network.

Possibility 1: Start reading blogs.
- Find a blog you like to read by using Google Blog Search: www.google.com/blogsearch.
- Set up an RSS feed to deliver that blog, as well as others, to Feedly, Flipboard, or another reading tool.
- When a blogger you like links to someone else, begin to follow that blog too.
- Provide comments and feedback on others' blog posts.

Possibility 2: Join Twitter and begin to participate in communities via hashtags.
- Sign up. Join Twitter and install one of their apps on your smartphone or tablet.
- Lurk. Explore the thousands of hashtags in use for various Twitter chats. For instance, NCTE has a regular chat using "#nctechat," and you can find more chats here: http://bit.ly/officialchatlist.
- Participate. Find out when the weekly, biweekly, or monthly focused chat time occurs. For instance, #nctechat happens on the third Sunday each month at 8:00 p.m. EST.
- Make connections. Follow people who participate in the chat and look for other related chat hashtags in their tweets.

Possibility 3: Reimagine social networks as reading and learning networks.
- Use your existing social networks to follow individuals, join groups, and share items of interest with other educators. For instance, both Kristen and Troy are members of a private group on Facebook specifically for English education professors, who often share links to relevant articles and resources.
- Join Goodreads or Shelfari with the specific goal of engaging in professional reading groups. For example, the group "YA Reads for Teachers (and Any Other Adults!)" on Goodreads enjoys both YA literature and professional books.
- Read and follow groups of educators, such as the Nerdy Book Club, who blog (http://nerdy bookclub.wordpress.com), tweet (#nerdybookclub), and participate as a group on Facebook (https://www.facebook.com/nerdybookclub).

in Figure 8.3 and suggested ideas for Connected Reading instruction. Conversations at the school level can focus on "here's what we already do" with an eye to shifting toward CRI, and we believe that individual efforts by teachers can snowball into wider reform.

In four decades of work, the National Writing Project (NWP) has sustained a successful model of teacher inquiry and professional development. Both of us have deep roots in the NWP (Kristen became a teacher consultant in 2002, Troy in 2003), and we adhere to their core principles in our own work with preservice and inservice teachers. Most notably, we agree that "teachers at every level—from kindergarten through college—are the agents of reform; universities and schools are ideal partners for investing in that reform through professional development" (National Writing Project, n.d.).

In the NWP model, teachers try out new ways of teaching in their own classrooms, develop research-based practices that work in their contexts, and share their own best practices with others who adapt the ideas to their contexts. "Teachers

Figure 8.3. Moving toward Connected Reading instruction (based on Zemelman, Daniels, & Hyde, 2012).

What we often see in good reading instruction	Instructional practices (and some tools) that we can imagine for use with Connected Reading
Time for independent, self-selected reading	• Teach students how to effectively browse for books (Goodreads, Shelfari, or a library website). • Curate a specific set of RSS feeds to deliver new reading material each day (Feedly, Flipboard). • Create a personal learning network (Twitter). • Create digital versions of book reviews.
Teacher modeling his or her own reading processes before, during, and after reading	• Record mini-lessons on specific reading strategies using screencasting tools. • Record a think-aloud of your own digital reading experiences with receiving, searching, surfing, and stumbling (TouchCast, Camtasia). • Demonstrate how you find and share reading materials using your PLN (Twitter, NCTE's Connected Community).
Focus on comprehension with opportunities to write before and after reading	• Share prompts for pre- and postreading via class website, text message, or social network. • Invite students to design their own polls and open-ended surveys about what they are reading (Poll Everywhere, SurveyMonkey, Google Forms). • Assign alternative writing assignments (Digital Book Trailers).
Social, collaborative activities with discussion and interest-based grouping	• Backchannel during class discussions (Twitter, TodaysMeet). • Use brainstorming tools (Gliffy, MindMeister, Popplet). • Invite shared annotations (Diigo, Subtext, Crocodoc, Ponder). • Collaborate on writing (Google Docs, Wikispaces).
Use of reading in content fields with instruction in disciplinary literacy	• Find, read, and share an Article of the Week (Feedly, Flipboard, Subtext). • Identify supplemental videos or materials to view before or after reading, shared on a class website.
Evaluation of higher-order thinking and a focus on students' attitudes toward reading	• Invite students, individually or in small groups, to record their thinking about a text as a screencast or VoiceThread. • Ask students to reflect on their reading and digital identities.

teaching teachers" allows for grassroots changes that are contextually based, not mandated from above. These changes stem from inquiry, and collaborative inquiry across contexts fuels the individual teacher's practice.

If you look beyond your local school, you will find many opportunities to connect with other educators and to conduct collaborative inquiry. Local NWP sites offer a variety of professional development opportunities directly to teachers in the form of courses, workshops, and conferences, as well as through teacher inquiry groups and teacher writing groups. At the national level, NWP offers a variety of resources to both foster PD and disseminate teacher research. Of particular note here, we point out the Digital Is website, http://digitalis.nwp.org, where you will find countless resources devoted to uses of digital reading and writing, as well as to principles of Connected Learning.

Other national organizations with which you might develop connections to support your PLN or your classroom practice are listed in Figure 8.4.

Figure 8.4. Organizations engaged in teaching, research, and policy decision making related to digital literacy learning.

Digital ID: 21st Century Citizenship	http://digital-id.wikispaces.com
Digital Media and Learning Research Hub	http://dmlhub.net
Digital Youth Network	www.digitalyouthnetwork.org
Edutopia	www.edutopia.org
Global Kids	www.globalkids.org
HASTAC: Humanities, Arts, Science, and Technology Alliance and Collaboratory	www.hastac.org
KQED's MindShift	http://blogs.kqed.org/mindshift
MacArthur Foundation's Digital Media and Learning	http://digitallearning.macfound.org
Mozilla's Hive Learning Network	http://hivenyc.org
NCTE's Connected Community	http://ncte.connectedcommunity.org/home
National Center for Literacy Education	www.literacyinlearningexchange.org
National Writing Project	www.nwp.org
National Writing Project's Digital Is	http://digitalis.nwp.org
New York Times Learning Network	http://learning.blogs.nytimes.com
TeachThought	www.teachthought.com

As you consider how Connected Reading can be shared through a variety of professional development contexts, from the individual to school-wide personnel to broader professional networks, we recommend building on current research, supporting individual teachers in their efforts to develop their own practices of Connected Reading, and considering the implications of what we do as readers in a digital age for instruction.

Call to Advocacy

As we redefine reading (and literacy) instruction, we need to consider how technology is adopted, how teachers develop their understandings, and the policies that guide acceptable use. First, rollouts must happen in smart, effective ways. Though we are encouraged by news that districts are providing one-to-one device access or adopting BYOD, we know that without consideration of how those devices allow teachers to redefine tasks and students to learn in ways not imagined before, these efforts will not amount to much.

To support rollouts of technology—and we do believe that adolescents need to learn with and through appropriate tools—teachers must work together to understand the evolving nature of literacy and how instruction affects learning. Policymakers (at both the national/state and local levels) can support the work that we outlined in the previous section by making resources available to teachers and students; but even more important, schools can do much of this work at a local level no matter what the nature (or lack thereof) of state or federal support. We recommend that administrators consider three areas as they create budgets and plan curricular initiatives: (1) providing connectivity, (2) allowing access, and (3) encouraging inquiry. We call on teachers to advocate that their districts adopt policies that help them move toward Connected Reading instruction.

1. Providing Connectivity

President Obama's ConnectED plan promises to provide 99 percent of students with high-speed Internet access in school by the year 2018, and these types of political initiatives are both important to and encouraging for CRI. It is imperative that students have widespread access to the Internet, and increasing bandwidth and wireless networks in a school building should be a focus of local decision making. These issues cross budget lines: they are related to curriculum, facilities, professional development, and general technology. Creativity in allocation and setting priorities that affect all of these areas are within local control.

Our current study also reveals that a large majority of teens possess wireless mobile devices, and through collaboration in the classroom and BYOD policies, full classes of students can learn with and through technology. Advocates of this approach suggest that students already have their own devices and should be allowed to use them. To a large extent, our research backs up the claim that students do have access to Internet-enabled devices. Critics of this approach, however, suggest that students who do not have their own devices will be even more disenfranchised. This is true, and we strongly encourage local schools and districts to think critically and creatively about ways they can work with community partners to get devices into the hands of all students. Organizations such as EveryoneOn (www.everyoneon.org) provide links to resources that can help local leaders in these efforts.

2. Allowing Access

We recognize the concerns about allowing students access to the Internet through a school's network. Kristen remembers vividly when a student used the computer in her classroom to hack into the system and send inappropriate messages under a teacher's account. The student was disciplined in accordance with the school's acceptable use policy, which outlined rules for computer and Internet use and held students accountable for their inappropriate actions. Over the last decade, however, we have seen AUPs continuously revised (and narrowed) as schools block particular websites. Many schools ban mobile devices for fear that stu-

dents will be distracted from learning. We see these as issues of classroom management (which teachers need to develop just as they always
have) and self-monitoring (which students need to develop as Connected
Readers).

We urge schools to reconsider AUPs to allow students to go online
and to access the sites that help them learn from a network of individuals
and via devices that they use comfortably. As Troy argues in a forthcom-
ing collection on new directions in teaching English,

> We would never stand for a school that limited access to pencils, paper,
> and books. So, too, must we never stand for a school—even in these times
> of limited budgets, core standards, and ongoing assessments—that would
> limit access to the Internet, prevent students from using the devices that
> they already use, or narrow our curricular scope and instructional choices.
> (Hicks, in press)

English teachers have always been advocates. We passionately argue
against banned books and for the diverse voices of our students. And
now we must advocate for digital literacy because the implications for
students are increasingly important. One useful resource for this effort
is the Consortium for School Networking's "Rethinking Acceptable
Use Policies to Enable Digital Learning: A Guide for School Districts"
(2013) in which they argue that "current educational context is characterized by expanded ownership of mobile devices and increased number
of interactive and collaborative applications and sites on the Internet"
and that districts must reshape AUPs accordingly. The guide, of course,
includes many suggestions and resources for doing so.

3. Encouraging Inquiry

These recommendations imply broad changes in the way we teach, and
it is important for teachers to be evaluated on their inquiries and not just
on student outcomes. Inquiry is a stance, and it involves experimentation
and reflection with the understanding that failure propels us forward.
Evaluation of inquiry is ongoing. It involves collecting many kinds of
data, discussing process, and allowing teachers to celebrate both their
successes and their failures—and to share how their inquiry will shape
future instruction. Test scores that are not immediately shared with
teachers so that they can alter instruction based on the needs of their
students should not be used to evaluate teachers. This practice does not
foster inquiry, and it will undermine a move toward CRI.

We feel fortunate to have worked with teachers who engaged in
inquiry during our study. They helped us to understand the challenges
in the classrooms that all teachers might face, and many of them truly
transformed their practice based on the results of the Connected Reading
lessons. Several of them advocated for local policy changes based on their
work.

For instance, Kaitlyn, who adapted our "Reflecting on Reading"
lesson by having her students analyze data using a Looking at Data pro-

tocol, used her students' survey results to argue for change in her school. She reflects:

> This data was helpful evidence in a meeting with administration about digital literacy in the classroom. As teachers, we have to be advocating for more and more individualized, student-based approaches to technology in our classrooms. Citing the responses from the Digital Literacy survey and the data collected, we have been approved for the purchase and use of iPads in our reading classes. I feel this is a major victory in our school in the adaptation of digital resources to improve and promote literacy.

Kaitlyn's success at advocating for her students and for their digital literacy is but one example of individual teachers leading the charge to changes in policy in their schools. We hope that the data we have shared in this book, as well as the instructional practices that rethink reading instruction, will inspire you to do the same.

Be an Advocate

Each of these three calls to action—providing connectivity, allowing access, and encouraging inquiry—could easily be added to the list of "not my job." As we noted earlier, however, "Over the years, teachers of English have rallied against censorship, fought for the inclusion of diverse voices in the canon of literature, and recognized the power of out-of-school literacies." Advocacy, in this sense, is a core part of what it means to teach reading, writing, and literacy more broadly.

Although what we have discovered for ourselves through our research confirms what Pew Internet has been reporting for years—more students have devices and access than ever before—our role as advocates must move well beyond helping students get tablets or laptops, though this is a big part of the process; reading on a device obviously requires that students have a device. Yet Connected Reading requires us to adopt a new instructional mindset, too. We are teaching students how to read, write, and participate in civil discourse. We are modeling for them how to find, interpret, and share evidence in their networks. We engage in Connected Reading to make ourselves and our peers better readers, writers, and thinkers.

In a practical sense, this shift means that budgets for instructional materials, as slim as they are these days, must be reallocated to purchasing devices as well as the applications and subscriptions to access digital texts. Textbook budgets, while still being deployed in smart ways, can also be used to connect students to high-quality digital resources. More important, we can use limited funds to purchase devices that mirror tablet screens wirelessly, such as the Apple TV and iPad or the Chromecast, without making huge investments in Smartboards. The goal is for teachers to model their own reading on screen, and we can do that relatively affordably with such devices.

Here are a few resources to consider as you investigate possibilities:

- Government websites:
    - EveryoneOn (www.everyoneon.org)
    - Computers for Learning (http://computersforlearning.gov)
- Directories of businesses selling refurbished technology:
    - Microsoft Registered Refurbisher (https://www.msregrefurb .com/RRPSite/OnlineDirectory.aspx)
    - TechSoup (www.techsoup.org)
- Nonprofits for refurbishing and donation:
    - Computers for Classrooms in Chico, California (http://www .computersforclassrooms.org)
    - Free Geek in Portland, Oregon (www.freegeek.org)
    - Operation: Kid Equip in Michigan (http://operationkidequip .org)
    - To find a nonprofit in your area, begin with a Web search for "donation computer education" and your city and/or state.

Reading Instruction for All, by All: Toward a Model of Connected Reading

As we reflect on our own inquiry into Connected Reading, we are left with a number of lingering questions that, we hope, teachers and researchers will take up in the next few years while a generation of students who came to kindergarten with tablets and smartphones in their hands are entering adolescence:

- What components of our Connected Reading model might evolve as technologies change and students develop reading skills independent of school?
- Within schools, how will assessments such as the SBAC and PARCC that require online reading affect instruction?
- What will happen as more and more states adopt open, online textbook projects (such as the type of program already in place in California)?
- How can we map—through eye-tracking software, MRI scans, and technologies yet to be invented—the actual process of reading digital texts and what happens in the meaning-making process?
- Ultimately, as teachers, how do we effectively develop the practices of Connected Readers?

We also have specific questions about multimodal texts and the practices of Connected Readers that we did not explore in this study. Though multimodal texts, particularly picture books, have been a part of conversations in English education for decades, Moje (2009) has called the field to rethink multimodality:

Consequently, it seems worth distinguishing between these closely related ideas of media themselves, uses of media, literate practices (or literacies), and the cognitive processes and social practices that derive from these uses of media and the practices for making sense of the texts offered by the media. The call for distinctions is not intended to reify categories, but to better understand how media, literacies, cognitive practices, and social practices overlap and are separate. (p. 351)

Research responding to Moje's call could be framed by our model of Connected Reading. Based on the data we collected, we believe that devices mediate interactions between the text and the reader and that specific text features have influence on the reader's comprehension. We hope researchers will respond to our call to explore our model more deeply and to elaborate on the practices of Connected Readers.

We also urge teachers to adopt a stance of inquiry in their classrooms and to share their learning with others. The Literacy in Learning Exchange (www .literacyinlearningexchange.org), a component of the National Center for Literacy Education, is a good place to find other teachers who share their stories, their practice, and their thinking about literacy and teaching.

We know that this book represents only a start to a line of inquiry, and more questions will arise in individual classrooms and at the broader professional level. We look forward to the ongoing, connected conversations that surround these questions. And, of course, reading about them across many print and digital texts.

We began this book by looking at the end of the *Reading Instruction for* All *Students* policy brief. It is worth reiterating that paragraph one more time:

Preparing students to read complex texts effectively is one of the most important and most challenging responsibilities of schools. With research-based support from policymakers and administration, teachers can enable students at all grade levels to comprehend, draw evidence from, and compare across a wide variety of complex texts.

Along with highlighting some of the theory and research that contributed to the thinking in this brief, we hope that our efforts at surveying and interviewing adolescent readers about the broader scope of their literacy practices have added a new layer of discussion to the conversation. We also hope that we have generatively complicated your understanding of what "complex texts" are, as well as offered productive ways for students to interact with a variety of print and digital texts.

From linear texts to nonlinear texts with links to multimedia, and across many devices and platforms, we know that students have ever-increasing opportunities for reading. Be it status messages, Web-based journalism, or ebooks, we know students are engaging with short-, mid-, and long-form texts. Each of these texts is complex in its own way, demanding different forms of attention and metacognition. We must, as we always have, teach students to monitor their own comprehension, yet we now must also teach them to be mindful and intentional in the ways they encounter, engage with, and evaluate what they read. By focusing on this concerted effort to move students toward more Connected Reading practices, we argue that engaging students in meaningful and motivational reading habits can occur alongside comprehension strategies and close reading instruction, in both print and digital forms of text.

As Sienna reminded us at the beginning of this chapter, "It's not so much about the books as it is about the stories, and I think books are a great platform to share stories." She, like us, sees the ways that a reader, a text, and a device can—with a nod to Rosenblatt (1978)—work together to make a new kind of poem. Various platforms allow us new opportunities for reading, and we must take advantage of them. With our efforts to use technologies such as ebooks, RSS readers, and social networks in conjunction with the principles of Connected Reading, we can live up to the promise of delivering reading instruction for all students.

Appendix A: Research Method

To find out *what*, *how*, and *why* teens read digitally, we worked with twelve middle and high school teachers during the spring and fall of 2013. We make specific reference to the year here because we acknowledge that in the changing landscape of digital literacies, data such as the kind we report here are never fixed. Still, in light of historical trends reported by the Pew Internet & American Life Project, on which our own survey was based, we see our data as complementary, reminding us that teens' use of the Internet and, more recently, mobile devices continues to rise year after year.

In various classrooms in Michigan, New Jersey, New York, and California, grades 7–12, we asked adolescents to reflect on their reading practices. We adapted the "Teen Parent Survey on Writing" used by the Pew Internet & American Life Project for their work related to writing, technology, and teens (Lenhart et al., 2008). We also interviewed adolescents about their reading practices. Finally, each of us taught one or more lessons related to digital literacy as we visited classrooms for two or three consecutive days or across an entire unit of study.

We took field notes and wrote reflective memos as part of this work. We also informally interviewed our teaching colleagues about their experiences during our lessons, as well as their own lessons for which we were not present. Furthermore, we interviewed individuals (authors and teachers) whom we met via Twitter during the course of our study in order to understand their reading practices, as well as the work they do with teens.

Most of the teachers in our study used our Digital Reading Survey (Appendix B provides an adaptation of this survey for broader classroom use) as part of regular class instruction (described in Chapter 6), and therefore we were fortunate to receive 804 responses that helped to create a picture of teens' access to technology, the nature of their reading, and their attitudes toward digital reading. We analyzed these data in a variety of ways, using the SPSS Statistics program to disaggregate by gender, geography, and grade range (middle or high school). We found few significant differences in the disaggregated data, but we do note any interesting ones through endnotes in this book.

In addition to collecting data from teens via surveys, we interviewed twenty-three individual students. Inspired by the work of Smith and Wilhelm (2002), we wrote fictional profiles of adolescent readers (Appendix C) and asked the teens to consider the following questions:

- What, if anything, do you admire about the character in the profile?

- What, if anything, do you not admire about the character in the profile?

- Where do you see yourself in the characters?

We found that once teens started talking about Sally, Maggie, Robin, Tabitha, or Alexandra (or their male counterparts), they easily reflected on their own reading practices, and we transcribed more than 650 minutes of conversation with the students.

We acknowledge the work of Smith and Wilhelm, which served as the methodological inspiration for our study. In their study of adolescent boys, Smith and Wilhelm (2002, 2006) examined out-of-school literacy practices, focusing on the motivational factors that encouraged reading, writing, and participation. Drawing from flow theory (Csikszentmihalyi, 1990) and their data collected from forty-nine interviews, Smith and Wilhelm suggested four principles that impact motivation:

- A sense of competence and control

- A challenge that requires an appropriate level of skill

- Clear goals and feedback
- A focus on the immediate experience

The stories of the boys in their study also suggested a fifth element that highly affects motivation to read (or write, or participate): the importance of the social. The participants suggested that the motivational factors present in their out-of-school lives did not exist in school. For them, the disconnect was obvious.

Smith and Wilhelm's (2002, 2006) work was groundbreaking in the sense that it brought several fields of research together. By focusing on motivation, academic literacy, and out-of-school literate lives, the researchers were able to offer a framework that highlighted "what readers do" and connect it to questions about "how we teach reading." We saw our questions as building from their findings. A decade later, we are presented with a new set of challenges. The tools and opportunities for reading have evolved exponentially, and teen readers are adapting to the opportunities, demands, and constraints of digital reading. Building on the research provided by Smith and Wilhelm, we sought to uncover what these young digital readers do and how we might teach them.

Therefore, we initially adopted Smith and Wilhelm's (2002, 2006) coding scheme for our own analysis. However, we quickly realized that something different was happening in our data, and we began a new process of coding inductively. Borrowing from grounded theory methodology (Charmaz, 2011), we examined the transcripts closely in a phase of *open coding*, using the words of the participants to generate labels, and then we grouped these codes into larger concepts. For example, "highlighting" was grouped with other similar codes into "annotating." We coded all of the data using the *selective* codes in the following chart and began to develop categories such as "Reading Practices" and "Reader Attributes."

Selective Codes

Reading Affect	Identity	Reading the Text
Negative		Scrolling
Positive	Apps	Readability
		Visual Layout
School Reading		Audio/Video
Negative	Types of Texts	Hyperlinks
Positive	Short-form	Skimming/Scanning
Tasks	Mid-form	Navigation
	Long-form	Platform/Tool
Flow		Cost
Competence	Digital Age Considerations	Multitasking
Challenge	Abundance	Efficiency
Immediate Experience	Access	Annotation
Social Activity		Searching
Goals/Feedback		Further Reading
		Distraction

At this point, we turned back to the literature on reading processes and instruction in reading to help us understand our data. Realizing that we were beginning to develop a unique model of what readers do, we stepped back from the data to engage in self-study by blogging publicly (Troy) and journaling privately (Kristen) about our own practices as digital readers. We undertook this work for a few reasons. First, we hoped to articulate what "expert" readers do when they read digitally since this kind of research has yet to be published. Second, we wanted to put forth our own biases as teachers and researchers and allow others to comment on them. This form of peer review allowed us to check our interpretations of the data as we worked with it.

Ultimately, the data led us to our model of Connected Reading, and we identified *theoretical* codes that included each area of our model, as well as the Connected Reading practices of encountering, engaging, and evaluating and their subcategories. We tested these codes in our own data and shared the model with teachers, researchers, and authors for feedback. As theory-building research, this study has started us on a path to investigating more fully the processes of readers in a digital age.

Appendix B: Digital Reading Survey, Classroom Version[3]

Name:[4]

School:

Teacher:

Period:

Gender:

Grade:

Internet and Device Use

Do you have a connection to the Internet at home?
- ❏ Yes
- ❏ No

Do you have a computer at home that can access the Internet?
- ❏ Yes
- ❏ No

Do you ever use the Internet from your own smartphone (e.g., BlackBerry, iPhone, Android)?
- ❏ Yes
- ❏ No

Do you have your own dedicated e-reader device (e.g., Kindle or Nook with no email, games, etc.)?
- ❏ Yes
- ❏ No

Do you have your own Internet-enabled device that is handheld (e.g., iPod Touch, PSP, Nintendo DS)?
- ❏ Yes
- ❏ No

Do you have your own tablet (e.g., Kindle Fire, Galaxy, iPad, Surface)?
- ❏ Yes
- ❏ No

A template version of this survey can be found on our wiki.

Overall, how often do you go online? (This might include playing games, chatting, video chatting, watching videos, reading articles, using social networks, and many other activities that take place via the Internet.)
- ❏ Several times a day
- ❏ About once a day
- ❏ 3–5 days a week
- ❏ 1–2 days a week
- ❏ Every few weeks
- ❏ Never
- ❏ Don't know

Social Networking
Which accounts do you have? Check all that apply.
- ❏ Facebook
- ❏ Twitter
- ❏ Instagram
- ❏ Google+
- ❏ Pinterest
- ❏ Other:

What social network account do you use the MOST?
- ❏ Facebook
- ❏ Twitter
- ❏ Instagram
- ❏ Google+
- ❏ Pinterest
- ❏ Other:

With this account that you use the MOST, how often do you use this network to discuss reading?
- ❏ All the time
- ❏ Quite often
- ❏ Occasionally
- ❏ Very infrequently
- ❏ Not at all

Do you have a social network account on a site devoted to reading, such as Goodreads or Shelfari?
- ❏ Yes
- ❏ No

Do you have an account on a site devoted to reading and fan fiction, such as Quotev, Wattpad, or FanFiction.Net?
- ❏ Yes
- ❏ No

Digital Reading Outside School
Think about the reading you do for yourself, NOT for school.

Do you read content from the Internet such as news stories, blog posts, or other material, at least occasionally?
- ❏ Yes
- ❏ No

Do you read digital books or magazines, at least occasionally?
- ❏ Yes
- ❏ No

Please check any of the items that you have read digitally OUTSIDE OF SCHOOL.
- ❏ News articles
- ❏ Journals
- ❏ Essays
- ❏ Blogs
- ❏ Any type of fiction, classic or contemporary
- ❏ Any type of nonfiction, classic or contemporary
- ❏ Poetry, plays, or other expressive works
- ❏ Music and lyrics
- ❏ Letters, messages, notes from other people
- ❏ Text messages, tweets, or other short digital posts.

Thinking about when you are reading for yourself and NOT for school, do you usually read on paper or do you read using an electronic device?
- ❏ Usually on paper
- ❏ Usually on electronic device
- ❏ A mixture, depending on situation
- ❏ Don't know

How much do you enjoy the reading you do just for yourself?
- ❏ A great deal
- ❏ Some
- ❏ Not much
- ❏ Not at all
- ❏ I don't read unless it's for school
- ❏ Don't know

Do you think of reading text messages, email, IMs, or social networking posts as READING?
- ❏ Yes
- ❏ No

Digital Reading in School
Please check any of the items that you have read digitally as part of your SCHOOL WORK.
- ❏ News articles
- ❏ Journals
- ❏ Essays
- ❏ Blogs
- ❏ Any type of fiction, classic or contemporary

- ❏ Any type of nonfiction, classic or contemporary
- ❏ Poetry, plays, or other expressive works
- ❏ Music and lyrics
- ❏ Letters, messages, notes from other people
- ❏ Text messages, tweets, or other short digital posts.

When you complete schoolwork, do you usually read on paper or do you read on an electronic device?
- ❏ Usually on paper
- ❏ Usually on electronic device
- ❏ A mixture, depending on situation
- ❏ Don't know

For which classes do you read on an electronic device?
- ❏ English
- ❏ Social studies
- ❏ Math
- ❏ Science
- ❏ Music
- ❏ Phys ed
- ❏ Art
- ❏ Media/Computer
- ❏ Other:

Do you read on electronic devices during school hours?
- ❏ Yes
- ❏ No

How much do you enjoy the reading that you do for school?
- ❏ A great deal
- ❏ Some
- ❏ Not much
- ❏ Not at all
- ❏ Don't know

If your teachers were able to use more computer-based tools to teach reading—such as games, reading help programs and websites, or multimedia—do you think this would help improve your reading skills?
- ❏ Yes
- ❏ No
- ❏ I don't know

Reading Skills and Interest
Do you read more when you can read on an electronic device?
- ❏ Read more because of device
- ❏ Read less because of device
- ❏ Makes no difference
- ❏ I never read on an electronic device
- ❏ I don't know

In the past year, do you think your reading skills have improved, gotten worse, or stayed the same?
- ❏ Skills improved
- ❏ Skills have gotten worse
- ❏ Little or no change
- ❏ I don't know

Do you think using electronic devices makes students more or less likely to READ BETTER OVERALL?
- ❏ More likely
- ❏ Less likely
- ❏ Makes no difference
- ❏ I don't know

Do you think using electronic devices makes students more or less likely to be INTERESTED in what they read?
- ❏ More likely
- ❏ Less likely
- ❏ Makes no difference
- ❏ I don't know

If you had to choose, which do you prefer:
- ❏ Reading a print text
- ❏ Reading on an electronic device

Open-Ended Questions
Imagine you are sitting at the computer or holding your smartphone or tablet and you are about to read something. What is most likely on your screen?

If you want to find something different to read than what is on your screen, how do you do it and how do you decide what to read?

With digital texts, you can make many choices about how to interact with a text (e.g., clicking links, looking up definitions, watching videos). How do these digital opportunities affect your reading?

If you come across a difficult text when you are reading on a computer or electronic device, what do you do to help you understand what you are reading?

Many people share links to articles with friends or family, post reviews of books on websites, or make comments about something they have read on social networks. How do you share your reading with other people?

As you have completed this survey, what else has come to mind about your habits as a digital reader? Please tell me anything else you think I should know.

Appendix C: Fictional Reader Profiles Used for Interviews

Profiles Used with Female Interviewees

Alexandra

Alexandra loves books and her last year's English teacher assigned novels that she enjoyed reading. This year, however, her teachers seem to be assigning more and more online reading and fewer books. Recently, her social studies teacher asked her to find news stories with an RSS tool, Google Reader, and she would have much rather looked at newspapers or magazines. She doesn't understand why all of her friends want Kindles and iPads when her school has a great library. She does do some social networking because she posts her book reviews on Goodreads, but she prefers to have an actual book in her hand as compared to another device.

Maggie

Maggie enjoys keeping up with her friends on a variety of social websites, including Facebook, Twitter, and Pinterest. While she spends most of her time scrolling through posts and offering comments, every once in a while she will click on a link to view a video or read a story that one of her friends has posted. She posts links to stories that she finds interesting, most often about movies and music. She uses her smartphone to get assignments from school websites, but she rarely reads novels unless it is required. Maggie is very close to her grandmother, who lives in another state, and they keep in touch via email, which she checks every day.

Robin

Robin has discovered that there are many apps she can use to read news about her latest passion: gaming. After a friend introduced her to World of Warcraft, she wanted to learn strategies for the game, and she has been reading online discussion boards via her smartphone. She loves playing games on her phone, particularly ones that have interesting characters and plots. She also likes social apps where she can connect with her friends and family. She doesn't understand why teachers can't use some of these ideas in school; games tell stories, too. Her mom in particular likes word games, and Robin enjoys chatting with her as they play Words with Friends.

Sally

Sally got her first Kindle two years ago, and she has borrowed a number of books from the public library and even more from Amazon's lending library. Periodically, she will use some of the money she earns babysitting to buy a particular book that she has enjoyed and knows she will want to read again later. As she reads her ebooks, she uses the dictionary feature to identify words that she doesn't understand. She also shares quotes from the books she reads on Goodreads.com so she and her friends can talk about the stories they enjoy. While she does do some reading on the Web, she regularly reads teen magazines that come in the mail. She is hoping to get the new Kindle Fire so she can subscribe to her magazines digitally.

Tabitha

Tabitha is a fan of both the Harry Potter and the Twilight series, having read each of the books at least twice. She loves to read fan fiction stories on the Web about the characters in these books, and since she got an iPad last year, she has begun to compose some of her own stories. She often provides feedback to other writers and enjoys sharing links to her work through Facebook. More recently, she found a website called "Inanimate

Alice," which is a transmedia story that includes images, music, text, games, and short videos to create chapters in a Web-based novel. She enjoys this type of multimodal experience and is trying to figure out how to create her own transmedia story. While she rarely checks news sites, she does have Yahoo as her homepage, and every time she opens her Web browser, she reads the news headlines.

Profiles Used with Male Interviewees

Andy

Andy loves books and his last year's English teacher assigned novels that he enjoyed reading. This year, however, his teachers seem to be assigning more and more online reading and fewer books. Recently, his social studies teacher asked him to find news stories with an RSS tool, Google Reader, and he would have much rather looked at newspapers or magazines. He doesn't understand why all of his friends want Kindles and iPads when his school has a great library. He does do some social networking because he posts his book reviews on Goodreads, but he prefers to have an actual book in his hand as compared to another device.

Max

Max enjoys keeping up with his friends on a variety of social websites, including Facebook, Twitter, and Pinterest. While he spends most of his time scrolling through posts and offering comments, every once in a while he will click on a link to view a video or read a story that one of his friends has posted. He posts links to stories that he finds interesting, most often about movies and music. He uses his smartphone to get assignments from school websites, but he rarely reads novels unless it is required. Max is very close to his grandfather, who lives in another state, and they keep in touch via email, which he checks every day.

Randy

Randy has discovered that there are many apps he can use to read news about his latest passion: gaming. After a friend introduced him to World of Warcraft, he wanted to learn strategies for the game, and he has been reading online discussion boards via his smartphone. He loves playing games on his phone, particularly ones that have interesting characters and plots. He also likes social apps where he can connect with his friends and family. He doesn't understand why teachers can't use some of these ideas in school; games tell stories, too. His brother in particular likes word games, and Randy enjoys chatting with him as they play Words with Friends.

Steven

Steven got his first Kindle two years ago, and he has borrowed a number of books from the public library and even more from Amazon's lending library. Periodically, he will use some of the money he earns to buy a particular book that he has enjoyed and knows he will want to read again later. As he reads ebooks, he uses the dictionary feature to identify words that he doesn't understand. He also shares quotes from the books he reads on Goodreads.com so he and his friends can talk about the stories they enjoy. While he does do some reading on the Web, he regularly reads magazines that come in the mail. He is hoping to get the new Kindle Fire so he can subscribe to magazines digitally.

Tito

Tito is a fan of the Lord of the Rings series, having read each of the books at least twice. He loves to read fan fiction stories on the Web about the characters in these books, and since he got an iPad last year, he has begun to compose some of his own stories. He often provides feedback to other writers and enjoys sharing links to his work through Facebook. More recently, he found a website called "Inanimate Alice," which is a transmedia story that includes images, music, text, games, and short videos to create chapters in a Web-based novel. He enjoys this type of multimodal experience and is trying to figure out how to create his own transmedia story. While he rarely checks news sites, he does have Yahoo as his homepage, and every time he opens his Web browser, he reads the news headlines.

Notes

1. There was a difference between middle and high school students for this question. While only three-quarters of middle school students answered yes, nine-tenths of high school students admitted to reading news stories and blogs.

2. Fifty-seven percent of females and 43 percent of males read digital books and magazines.

3. We modeled our survey on one designed for the 2008 Pew Internet report, and we stayed close to the questions asked in that study in the version we administered. This version is adapted for ease of classroom use and pares down the data to those items that we feel will best contribute to reflection on reading habits.

4. Per our Institutional Review Board approvals, we did not collect student names in our survey. Each student entered a random ID number and was classified by school, teacher, and class period.

Annotated Bibliography

As you continue your journey toward becoming a Connected Reader and teaching Connected Reading to your students, we encourage you to view our wiki (connectedreading.wikispaces.com), where we have links to many of the articles, books, and Web texts discussed in this book. Here we highlight just a few of the many available resources that deserve particular attention.

Pew Internet (www.pewinternet.org)

The Pew Research center, a trusted, nonpartisan organization, has been tracking Internet demographics since 2001. They research various demographic groups, including teenagers, and provide numerous reports related to Internet (and technology) use among these demographics, including those we cite in the book. They have a number of interactive tools that could be useful in the classroom or in professional development.

Digital Media and Learning Research Hub (dmlhub.net)

Supported by the MacArthur Foundation, the Digital Media and Learning Research Hub sponsors a variety of research projects and initiatives related to digital learning, the maker movement, and open education resources. Researchers affiliated with DML Hub include Howard Gardner, James Gee, Kris Gutierrez, Mimi Ito, and Henry Jenkins. DML Hub partners with the National Writing Project, and it is part of the Connected Learning Initiative. In addition to the report we cite in this book, *Connected Learning: An Agenda for Research and Design* (Ito et al., 2013), DML Hub has released a number of other free resources, most notably *Hanging Out, Messing Around, and Geeking Out: Kids Living and Learning with New Media* (2009).

The Text Review Forum: Visual and Digital Texts (www.reading.org/general/Publications/Journals/JAAL.aspx)

Described as a column that "provides reviews of adolescent and adult visual and digital texts and provides a valuable resource for visual and digital text selection in and outside the classroom," the Visual and Digital Texts section of the Text Review Forum provides readers of the *Journal of Adolescent & Adult Literacy* with timely and useful texts for both students and teachers' own professional learning. The journal is published by the International Reading Association, and a subscription is required to access it.

The Debate about Online Reading and Engagement

We refer throughout the book to an ongoing debate about the effects of technology on our ability to stay focused, read deeply, and, ultimately, engage with texts. On one side of the debate are scholars and journalists such as Mark Bauerlein and Nicholas Carr who argue that the effects of digital media are negative. These effects include shortened attention spans; lack of interest in reading longer texts, especially novels; and an inability to remember information from our reading.

Bauerlein, M. (2008). *The dumbest generation: How the digital age stupefies young Americans and jeopardizes our future.* New York: Tarcher/Penguin.

Carr, N. (2010). *The shallows: What the Internet is doing to our brains.* New York: Norton.

On the other side of the debate, scholars and journalists such as Clive Thompson and Howard Rheingold argue that digital media is in fact helping us to become more conscious and connected readers. While they acknowledge the role that distraction can play, they also advocate for mindful uses of technology, which include taking advantage of new ways to access and annotate texts, sharing reading with a social network, and understanding the affordances and constraints of multimedia.

Rheingold, H. (2012). *Net smart: How to thrive online*. Cambridge, MA: MIT Press.

Thompson, C. (2013). *Smarter than you think: How technology is changing our minds for the better*. New York: Penguin.

To be certain, this debate will continue. Sites like ProCon have issue pages set up for Tablets vs. Textbooks (http://tablets-textbooks.procon.org/), and stories about e-reading continue to fill the news.

For more resources, please visit our wiki: http://connectedreading.wikispaces.com.

References

Atwell, N. (2007). *The reading zone: How to help kids become skilled, passionate, habitual, critical readers.* New York: Scholastic.

Baron, D. (2001). From pencils to pixels: The stages of literacy technology. In E. Cushman, E. R. Kintgen, B. M. Kroll, & M. Rose (Eds.), *Literacy: A critical sourcebook* (pp. 70–84). Boston: Bedford/St. Martin's. Retrieved from http://www.english.illinois.edu/-people-/faculty/debaron/essays/pencils.htm

Bauerlein, M. (2008). *The dumbest generation: How the digital age stupefies young Americans and jeopardizes our future (or, don't trust anyone under 30).* New York: Tarcher/Penguin.

Beach, R., Anson, C., Breuch, L.-A. K., & Swiss, T. (2008). *Teaching writing using blogs, wikis, and other digital tools.* Norwood, MA: Christopher-Gordon.

Beers, K. (2003). *When kids can't read, what teachers can do: A guide for teachers, 6–12.* Portsmouth, NH: Heinemann.

Beers, K., & Probst, R. E. (2012). *Notice and note: Strategies for close reading.* Portsmouth, NH: Heinemann.

Benjamin, A. (2013). *Formative assessment for English language arts: A guide for middle and high school teachers.* Hoboken, NJ: Taylor and Francis.

Bolter, J. D. (2001). *Writing space: Computers, hypertext, and the remediation of print* (2nd ed.). New York: Routledge.

Branch, J. (2012). Snow fall: The avalanche at Tunnel Creek. Retrieved from http://www.nytimes.com/projects/2012/snow-fall/

Brummett, B. (2009). *Techniques of close reading.* London: SAGE.

Canada, G. (2010). *Fist, knife, stick, gun: A personal history of violence.* Boston: Beacon Press.

Carnegie Corporation of New York's Council on Advancing Adolescent Literacy. (2009). Time to act: An agenda for advancing adolescent literacy for college and career success. New York: Carnegie Corporation of New York. Retrieved from http://carnegie.org/publications/search-publications/pub/195/

Carr, N. (2008, July 1). Is Google making us stupid? What the internet is doing to our brains. *The Atlantic.* Retrieved from http://www.theatlantic.com/magazine/archive/2008/07/is-google-making-us-stupid/6868/

Carr, N. (2010). *The shallows: What the Internet is doing to our brains.* New York: Norton.

Carroll, L. (1865). *Alice's adventures in Wonderland.* London: Macmillan.

Cart, M. (2010). *Young adult literature: From romance to realism.* Chicago: American Library Association.

Charmaz, K. (2011). *Constructing grounded theory: A practical guide through qualitative analysis.* Los Angeles: SAGE.

Cochran-Smith, M., & Lytle, S. L. (2009). *Inquiry as stance: Practitioner research in the next generation.* New York: Teachers College Press.

Coiro, J. (2005). Reading comprehension: Making sense of online text. *Educational Leadership, 63*(2), 30–35.

Coiro, J. (2011). Talking about reading as thinking: Modeling the hidden complexities of online reading comprehension. *Theory Into Practice, 50*(2), 107–115. doi:10.1080/00405841.2011.558435

Coiro, J., & Kennedy, C. (2011). The online reading comprehension assessment (ORCA) project: Preparing students for common core standards and 21st century literacies. Retrieved from http://www.academia.edu/931282/Coiro_J._and_Kennedy_C._2011_._The_online_reading_comprehension_assessment_ORCA_project_Preparing_students_for_common_core_standards_and_21st_century_literacies._White_paper_based_on_work_supported_by_the_United_States_Department_of_Education_under_Award_No._R305G050154_and_R305A090608

Common Core State Standards Initiative. (2010). *Common core state standards for English language arts and literacy in history/social studies, science, and technical subjects.* Retrieved from http://www.corestandards.org/ELA-Literacy/

Consortium for School Networking. (2013, March). *Rethinking acceptable use policies to enable digital learning: A guide for school districts.* Retrieved from http://www.cosn.org/sites/default/files/pdf/Revised%20AUP%20March%202013_final.pdf

Csikszentmihalyi, M. (1990). *Flow: The psychology of optimal experience.* New York: Harper and Row.

Dalton, B., & Proctor, C. P. (2008). The changing landscape of text and comprehension in the age of new literacies. In J. Coiro, M. Knobel, C. Lankshear, & D. J. Leu (Eds.), *Handbook of research on new literacies* (pp. 297–324). New York: Taylor and Francis.

Daniels, H. (2002). *Literature circles: Voice and choice in book clubs and reading groups* (2nd ed.). Portland, ME: Stenhouse.

Daniels, H., & Steineke, N. (2011). *Texts and lessons for content-area reading: With more than 75 articles from* The New York Times, Rolling Stone, The Washington Post, Car and Driver, Chicago Tribune, *and many others.* Portsmouth, NH: Heinemann.

Daniels, H., & Zemelman, S. (2004). *Subjects matter: Every teacher's guide to content-area reading.* Portsmouth, NH: Heinemann.

Daniels, H., Zemelman, S., & Steineke, N. (2007). *Content-area writing: Every teacher's guide.* Portsmouth, NH: Heinemann.

Davidson, C. N. (2011). *Now you see it: How the brain science of attention will transform the way we live, work, and learn.* New York: Viking.

Eagleton, T. (2008). *Literary theory: An introduction.* Minneapolis: University of Minnesota Press.

Fisher, D., Brozo, W. G., Frey, N., & Ivey, G. (2010). *50 instructional routines to develop content literacy* (2nd ed.). New York: Pearson.

Fisher, D., & Frey, N. (2007). *Checking for understanding: Formative assessment techniques for your classroom.* Alexandria, VA: ASCD.

Fisher, D., & Frey, N. (2011). *Improving adolescent literacy: Content area strategies at work* (3rd ed.). New York: Pearson.

Fisher, D., & Frey, N. (2013). What's the secret to successful close reading? Strategic preparation and follow up. *Reading Today, 31*(2), 16–17.

Fleming, L. (2013). Expanding learning opportunities with transmedia practices: Inanimate Alice as an exemplar. *Journal of Media Literacy Education,* *5*(2), 370–377. Retrieved from http://digital commons.uri.edu/jmle/vol5/iss2/3

Gallagher, K. (2009). *Readicide: How schools are killing reading and what you can do about it.* Portland, ME: Stenhouse.

Gere, A. R., Homan, E. C., Parsons, C., Spooner, R. A., & Uzogara, C. (2014). *Text complexity: Supporting student readers, grades 9–12.* Urbana, IL: National Council of Teachers of English.

Gunter, G., & Kenny, R. (2008). Digital booktalk: Digital media for reluctant readers. *Contemporary Issues in Technology and Teacher Education, 8*(1). Retrieved from http://www.citejournal.org/vol14/iss3/

Hagerman, M. S., & White, A. (2013). What's the best formula for enhancing online inquiry skills? [(PST)^2 + (iC^3)]. *Reading Today, 31*(3), 20–21.

Harvey, S., & Goudvis, A. (2007). *Strategies that work: Teaching comprehension for understanding and engagement* (2nd ed.). Portland, ME: Stenhouse.

Hayn, J. A., & Kaplan, J. S. (Eds.). (2012). *Teaching young adult literature today: Insights, considerations, and perspectives for the classroom teacher.* Lanham, MD: Rowman and Littlefield.

Hicks, T. (2009). *The digital writing workshop.* Portsmouth, NH: Heinemann.

Hicks, T. (2013). *Crafting digital writing: Composing texts across media and genres.* Portsmouth, NH: Heinemann.

Hicks, T. (in press). (Digital) literacy advocacy: A rationale for creating shifts in policy, infrastructure, and instruction. In E. Morrell & L. Scherff (Eds.), *New directions in teaching English: Reimagining teaching, teacher education, and research.* Lanham, MD: Rowman & Littlefield.

Hicks, T., & Perrin, D. (2014). Beyond single modes and media: Writing as an ongoing multimodal text production. In E.-M. Jakobs & D. Perrin (Eds.), *Handbook of writing and text production* (Vol. 10, pp. 231–253). Berlin, Germany: Mouton de Gruyter.

Hicks, T., & Turner, K. H. (2013). No longer a luxury: Digital literacy can't wait. *English Journal, 102*(6), 58–65.

Hobbs, R. (2010). *Copyright clarity: How fair use supports digital learning.* Thousand Oaks, CA: Corwin Press.

Hudson, D. (2014, Feburary 4). President Obama visits a middle school classroom—and borrows a student's iPad. [Web Log Post]. Retrieved from http://www.whitehouse.gov/blog/2014/02/04/president-obama-visits-middle-school-classroom-and-borrows-student-s-ipad

Hyler, J., & Hicks, T. (2014). *Create, compose, connect! Reading, writing, and learning with digital tools.* New York: Routledge.

Hypertext. (2013, November 3). In *Wikipedia, the free encyclopedia*. Retrieved from https://en.wikipedia.org/w/index.php?title=Hypertext&oldid=580001557

International Reading Association. (2012a). *Adolescent literacy* (Position statement, Rev. ed.). Newark, DE: Author. Retrieved from http://www.reading.org/Libraries/resources/ps1079_adolescent literacy_rev2012.pdf

International Reading Association. (2012b). *Resolution on literacy assessment.* Newark, DE: Author. Retrieved from http://www.reading.org/Libraries/resources/On_Literacy_Assessment_Resolution.pdf

Ito, M., Gutiérrez, K., Livingstone, S., Penuel, B., Rhodes, J., Salen, K., . . . Watkins, S. C. (2013). *Connected learning: An agenda for research and design.* Irvine, CA: Digital Media and Learning Research Hub. Retrieved from http://clrn.dmlhub.net/publications/connected-learning-an-agenda-for-research-and-design

Itzkovitch, A. (2012, April 12). Interactive ebook apps: The reinvention of reading and interactivity. *UX Magazine*, Article No. 816. Retrieved from http://uxmag.com/articles/interactive-ebook-apps-the-reinvention-of-reading-and-interactivity

Jetton, T. L., & Shanahan, C. (Eds.). (2012). *Adolescent literacy in the academic disciplines: General principles and practical strategies.* New York: Guilford Press.

Kajder, S. (2010). *Adolescents and digital literacies: Learning alongside our students.* Urbana, IL: National Council of Teachers of English.

Kajder, S. B. (2006). *Bringing the outside in: Visual ways to engage reluctant readers.* Portland, ME: Stenhouse.

Keene, E. O., & Zimmermann, S. (2007). *Mosaic of thought: The power of comprehension strategy instruction* (2nd ed.). Portsmouth, NH: Heinemann.

Kidd, S. M. (2002). *The secret life of bees.* New York: Penguin.

Kist, W. (2005). *New literacies in action: Teaching and learning in multiple media.* New York: Teachers College Press.

Kittle, P. (2013). *Book love: Developing depth, stamina, and passion in adolescent readers.* Portsmouth, NH: Heinemann.

Knobel, M., & Lankshear, C. (2006). Profiles and perspectives: Discussing new literacies. *Language Arts, 84*(1), 78–86.

Kolb, L. (2008). *Toys to tools: Connecting student cell phones to education.* Washington DC: International Society for Technology in Education.

Kolb, L. (2011). *Cell phones in the classroom: A practical guide for educators.* Washington DC: International Society for Technology in Education.

Krashen, S. (2002). The Lexile Framework: The controversy continues. *California School Library Association Journal, 25*(2), 29–31.

Larson, L. C. (2009). e-Reading and e-responding: New tools for the next generation of readers. *Journal of Adolescent & Adult Literacy, 53*(3), 255–58. doi:10.1598/JAAL.53.3.7

Lee, H. (1960). *To kill a mockingbird.* Philadelphia: Lippincott.

Lehman, C., & Roberts, K. (2014). *Falling in love with close reading: Lessons for analyzing texts and life.* Portsmouth, NH: Heinemann.

Lenhart, A., Arafeh, S., Smith, A., & Macgill, A. (2008, April 24). *Writing, technology and teens.* Washington DC: Pew Internet and American Life Project. Retrieved from http://www.pewinternet.org/2008/04/24/writing-technology-and-teens/

Leu, D. J., Jr., Kinzer, C. K., Coiro, J., & Cammack, D. W. (2004). Toward a theory of new literacies emerging from the Internet and other information and communication technologies. In R. B. Ruddell, & N. Unrau (Eds.), *Theoretical models and processes of reading* (5th ed., pp. 1570–1613). Newark, DE: International Reading Association. Available: http://www.readingonline.org/new literacies/lit_index.asp?HREF=leu/

Miller, D. (2009). *The book whisperer: Awakening the inner reader in every child*. San Francisco, CA: Jossey-Bass.

Miller, D. (2012, July 25). Guess my Lexile [Web log post]. *Education Week: The Book Whisperer*. Retrieved from http://blogs.edweek.org/teachers/book_whisperer/2012/07/guess_my_lexile.html

Mitchell, D. (1998). Fifty alternatives to the book report. *English Journal, 87*(1), 92–95.

Moje, E. B. (2009). Standpoints: A call for new research on new and multi-literacies. *Research in the Teaching of English, 43*(4), 348–362.

Moje, E. B., Overby, M., Tysvaer, N., & Morris, K. (2008). The complex world of adolescent literacy: Myths, motivations, and mysteries. *Harvard Educational Review, 78*(1), 107–154.

Morsy, L., Kieffer, M., & Snow, C. (2010). *Measure for measure: A critical consumers' guide to reading comprehension assessments for adolescents*. New York: Carnegie Corporation of New York. Retrieved from http://carnegie.org/fileadmin/Media/Publications/PDF/tta_Morsy.pdf

National Commission on Excellence in Education. (1983, April). *A nation at risk: The imperative for educational reform*. Retrieved from http://datacenter.spps.org/uploads/SOTW_A_Nation_at_Risk_1983.pdf

National Council of Teachers of English. (2006, November). *Principles of professional development* (Position statement). Retrieved from http://www.ncte.org/positions/statements/profdevelopment

National Council of Teachers of English. (2013, October 21). *Formative assessment that* truly *informs instruction* (Position statement). Urbana, IL: Author.

National Council of Teachers of English, and International Reading Association. (2009). Standards for the assessment of reading and writing: Glossary of assessment terminology. In *Standards for the assessment of reading and writing* (Rev. ed.). Retrieved from http://www.ncte.org/standards/assessmentstandards/glossary#summative assessment

National Writing Project. (n.d.). *About NWP*. Retrieved from http://www.nwp.org/cs/public/print/doc/about.csp

National Writing Project (with DeVoss, D. N., Eidman-Aadahl, E., & Hicks, T.). (2010). *Because digital writing matters: Improving student writing in online and multimedia environments*. San Francisco, CA: Jossey-Bass.

Newkirk, T. (2012). *The art of slow reading: Six time-honored practices for engagement*. Portsmouth, NH: Heinemann.

Nielsen, L., & Webb, W. (2011). *Teaching generation text: Using cell phones to enhance learning*. San Francisco, CA: Jossey-Bass.

Pariser, E. (2011). *The filter bubble: What the internet is hiding from you*. New York: Penguin.

Patterson, N. G. (2000). Hypertext and the changing roles of readers. *The English Journal, 90*(2), 74–80.

Pearson, P. D., & Johnson, D. D. (1978). *Teaching reading comprehension*. Holt, Rinehart and Winston.

Prensky, M. (2001). Digital natives, digital immigrants (Part 1). *On the Horizon, 9*(5), 1–6. Retrieved from http://www.marcprensky.com/writing/Prensky%20-%20Digital%20Natives,%20Digital%20Immigrants%20-%20Part1.pdf

Puentedura, R. R. (2010). SAMR and TPCK: Intro to advanced practice. Retrieved from http://hippasus.com/resources/sweden2010/SAMR_TPCK_IntroToAdvancedPractice.pdf

Puentedura, R. R. (2014, January 31). *SAMR: An applied introduction*. Retrieved from http://www.hippasus.com/rrpweblog/archives/2014/01/31/SAMRAnAppliedIntroduction.pdf

Rheingold, H. (2012). *Net smart: How to thrive online*. Cambridge, MA: MIT Press.

Richardson, W. (2010). *Blogs, wikis, podcasts, and other powerful web tools for classrooms* (3rd ed.). Thousand Oaks, CA: Corwin Press.

Richardson, W., & Mancabelli, R. (2011). *Personal learning networks: Using the power of connections to transform education*. Bloomington, IN: Solution Tree Press.

Rosenblatt, L. M. (1978). *The reader, the text, the poem: The transactional theory of the literary work*. Carbondale, IL: Southern Illinois University Press.

Shanahan, T. (2012, June 18). What is close reading? [Web Log Post]. Retrieved from http://www.shanahanonliteracy.com/2012/06/what-is-close-reading.html

Shanahan, T., & Shanahan, C. (2008). Teaching disciplinary literacy to adolescents: Rethinking content-area literacy. *Harvard Educational Review*, *78*(1), 40–59.

Shirky, C. (2008). *Here comes everybody: The power of organizing without organizations.* New York: Penguin.

Shirky, C. (2011). *Cognitive surplus: How technology makes consumers into collaborators.* New York: Penguin.

Smith, M. W., & Wilhelm, J. D. (2002). *"Reading don't fix no Chevys": Literacy in the lives of young men.* Portsmouth, NH: Heinemann.

Smith, M. W., & Wilhelm, J. D. (2006). *Going with the flow: How to engage boys (and girls) in their literacy learning.* Portsmouth, NH: Heinemann.

Thompson, C. (2010, December 27). Clive Thompson on how tweets and texts nurture in-depth analysis. *Wired Magazine*. Retrieved from http://www.wired.com/magazine/2010/12/st_thompson_short_long/

Thompson, C. (2013). *Smarter than you think: How technology is changing our minds for the better.* New York: Penguin.

Thurlow, C. (2006). From statistical panic to moral panic: The metadiscursive construction and popular exaggeration of new media language in the print media. *Journal of Computer-Mediated Communication*, *11*(3), 667–701. doi:10.1111/j.1083-6101.2006.00031.x

Tovani, C. (2000). *I read it, but I don't get it: Comprehension strategies for adolescent readers.* Portland, ME: Stenhouse.

Tovani, C. (2004). *Do I really have to teach reading? Content comprehension, grades 6–12.* Portland, ME: Stenhouse.

Tovani, C. (2011). *So what do they really know? Assessment that informs teaching and learning.* Portland, ME: Stenhouse.

Turkle, S. (2011). *Alone together: Why we expect more from technology and less from each other.* New York: Basic Books.

Turner, K. H. (2009). Flipping the switch: Code-switching from text speak to standard English. *English Journal*, *98*(5), 60–65.

Turner, K. H. (2012). Digitalk as community. *English Journal*, *101*(4), 37–42.

Turner, K. H. (2014). Error or strength? Competencies developed in adolescent digitalk. In K. E. Pytash, & R. E. Ferdig (Eds.), *Exploring technology for writing and writing instruction* (pp. 114–134). Hershey, PA: IGI Global.

Twain, M. (2010). *The Adventures of Tom Sawyer.* Costa Mesa, CA: Saddleback Educational. (Original work published 1876)

Wesch, M. (2007, March 8). The machine is us/ing us (final version). [Video file]. Retrieved from https://www.youtube.com/watch?v=NLlGopyXT_g&feature=youtube_gdata_player

Wilhelm, J. D., & Friedemann, P. D. (with Erickson, J.). (1998). *Hyperlearning: Where projects, inquiry, and technology meet.* Portland, ME: Stenhouse.

Wilhelm, J. D., & Smith, M. W. (with Fransen, S.). (2014). *Reading unbound: Why kids need to read what they want—and why we should let them.* New York: Scholastic.

Wolf, S. A., Coats, K., Enciso, P., & Jenkins, C. A. (Eds.). (2011). *Handbook of research on children's and young adult literature.* New York: Taylor & Francis.

Zemelman, S., Daniels, H., & Hyde, A. (2012). *Best practice: Bringing standards to life in America's classrooms.* Portsmouth, NH: Heinemann.

Zickuhr, K., & Rainie, L. (2014, January 16). *E-reading rises as device ownership jumps.* Washington, DC: Pew Research Internet Project. Retrieved from http://www.pewinternet.org/2014/01/16/e-reading-rises-as-device-ownership-jumps/

Index

Authors

Kristen Hawley Turner is an associate professor of English education and contemporary literacies at Fordham University in New York City. Her research focuses on the intersections between technology and literacy, and she works with teachers across content areas to implement effective literacy instruction and to incorporate technology in meaningful ways. Turner is author of several journal articles and book chapters dealing with adolescent *digitalk*, technology and teacher education, and writing instruction, and she regularly provides professional development workshops related to literacy instruction for teachers. A former high school teacher of English and social studies, she is the director of the Fordham Digital Literacies Collaborative, a professional network for teachers in the NYC area, and a teacher consultant for the National Writing Project. Turner is the program coordinator for both the doctoral studies in Contemporary Learning and Interdisciplinary Research (CLAIR) and the master's program in English education at Fordham University. She can be found on Twitter @teachKHT, and she blogs about being a working mother of twins at http://twinlifehavingitall.blogspot.com.

Troy Hicks is an associate professor of English at Central Michigan University and focuses his work on the teaching of writing; literacy and technology; and teacher education and professional development. A former middle school teacher, he collaborates with K–12 colleagues and explores how they implement newer literacies in their classrooms. Hicks directs CMU's Chippewa River Writing Project, a site of the National Writing Project, and he frequently conducts professional development workshops related to writing and technology. Also, Hicks is author of *Crafting Digital Writing* (2013) and *The Digital Writing Workshop* (2009), coauthor of *Because Digital Writing Matters* (2010) and *Create, Compose, Connect!* (2014), as well as author of numerous journal articles and book chapters. In March 2011, he was honored with CMU's Provost's Award for junior faculty who have demonstrated outstanding achievement in research and creative activity. Hicks was also recognized by NCTE's Conference on English Education with the Richard Meade Award for research in English education in the fall of 2014. He blogs at Digital Writing, Digital Teaching and can be followed on Twitter @hickstro.

This book was typeset in Janson Text and BotonBQ by Barbara Frazier.

Typefaces used on the cover include American Typewriter, Frutiger Bold, Formata Light, and Formata Bold.

The book was printed on 60-lb. White Recycled Offset paper by Versa Press, Inc.